Penguin Special
The New Militants

KT-194-417

Paul Ferris, who also writes for newspapers and
television, is the author of five novels, and of a
number of books which report on aspects of the
present-day British scene. (They include *The City*,
The Church of England, *The Doctors*, *The Nameless*
and *Men and Money*. All available in Pelicans.)
He was born in 1929 in Wales and now lives in
London.

The New Militants:
Crisis in the Trade Unions

Paul Ferris

Penguin Books

Penguin Books Ltd, Harmondsworth,
Middlesex, England
Penguin Books Australia Ltd, Ringwood,
Victoria, Australia

Published in Penguin Books 1972

Copyright © Paul Ferris, 1972

Made and printed in Great Britain by
C. Nicholls and Company Ltd
Set in Monotype Times

Contents

1. A View of the Unions

Trade unions, like most institutions, complain that only their troubles are reported. Journalists neglect them when they proceed in orderly fashion, doing unnewsworthy things. 'Why don't you write about the shop stewards who *settle* disputes, not cause them?' they ask unhappily, knowing you won't. Jack Jones of the Transport and General Workers' Union told me over the telephone to direct my attention away from the docks and the motor-car industry, which I wanted to talk about, and look instead at the food industry or brewing, where they had excellent agreements. 'What about whisky?' he said. 'That's as important as cars.' I said I supposed he wasn't serious, but he swore that he was.

Most of the time, unions are not exciting. Eleven million citizens (out of 23 million at work) belong to them; recruits have hurried forward since 1968 to make up for lost time after the war, lifting union membership to its highest level. With their families, virtually half the nation is in the trade union camp.* Few workers are old-fashioned sons of toil; another decade or so, and there will be more in offices than factories. Older industries, like railways, coal mining and textiles, are in decline. Office and laboratory workers already account for two-fifths of the labour force, in and out of unions. Among union members, the white-collar proportion has risen rapidly, from a fifth after the war to a third today.

Unions grind ahead, generating claims, arguments, assistance,

*Where does the other half work? There are barely three-quarters of a million employers and self-employed. Managers and supervisors still have relatively few union members. Unions are weak in the distributive trades, catering and hotels, clothing, farming, insurance, banking and construction. Little more than half the $4\frac{1}{2}$ million in engineering and metal manufacture belong to unions Three-quarters of railwaymen are union members; so are nine out of ten coal miners.

advice, and sometimes anger, on behalf, so the rules of the game
assume, of the more or less underprivileged. The full-version
report of Jones's union, the largest in the country, is grey with
data from its eleven trade groups, reporting progress in clanking
prose full of 'revised structures', 'shift differentials' and 'minimum-time rates'. The union prints 20,000 or so copies; few
members would want to glance at one, except those whose shift
differentials or minimum-time rates had been affected. Trade
unions are relevant once they make money for you – or are seen
to be making it for somebody else, conceivably at your expense.

It is what colours the middle-class view of the unions. The
underprivileged are no longer the obviously weak, ground down
by the obviously strong. The middle classes have a nightmare.
Workers with cars and jeering expressions swarm through the
land, snatching new handfuls of the national cake. Governments
whimper and retreat. There is some justification for this view.
Miners and dockers have used their strength visibly to obtain
benefits that the Government thought extravagant. Both industries are moribund and full of fears, but this only partly
explains the mood. Workers are asserting themselves in a louder
voice. No doubt they are entitled to on moral grounds. But it is
a new phenomenon. The trade-union movement is more left-
wing than at any time in its history. The two largest unions, Jack
Jones's T G W U (1.6 million members) and Hugh Scanlon's Amalgamated Union of Engineering Workers (1.4 million) are
audibly militant. Jones and Scanlon would deny the unions are
'theirs'; each is elected and responsible to an executive. But they
reflect and in turn focus the mood of their members. This mood
is utterly different to the one that prevailed immediately after the
war. Opposition to the Industrial Relations Act has added
further ingredients. The idea of 'direct action', of using unions
for political ends, has revived after half a century.

All this has had a boisterous effect on radicals who see events
moving agreeably towards major unrest. This is how a leading
Communist, Bert Ramelson, the party's industrial organizer in
Britain, sees the situation. 'In a sense,' he says, 'the State has
created its own monster. After the war it tried more and more to
reach agreements at the top with right-wing union leaders. This

was tremendously important for us, the realization that it's no good having militants at the bottom and not at the top. So there was a move to change who's at the top. For the first time in its history there is now a very important minority of left-wingers at the TUC.'

The Communist Party didn't put them there; it just helped. It is not a plot but a process. But the core of many people's fears is that even 'respectable' trade-union leaders now advocate policies that plunge towards socialism via chaos. Hugh Scanlon, president of the AUEW, is the most familiar name in these uneasy speculations. The left-wing of the union put him into power, with strong Communist support. He tells an interviewer: 'Undoubtedly, the final role of the trade unions must be to change society itself, not merely to get the best out of existing society.'*

I put the proposition to him as I had heard it from a personnel director† in Manchester, a city where Scanlon's name rings daily in the employers' ears. The director had said: 'Hugh Scanlon is a likeable villain. He wants to cause disruption. He wants to cause chaos. He wants to squeeze industry out of existence, to make capitalism fail – to prove that it doesn't work. He then wants to drag socialism out of the ashes.'

Scanlon considered this for one second. He is a slightly-built man with eyes that fix themselves on the person he is speaking to; like many people from working-class backgrounds, he doesn't use the middle-class trick of constantly looking away from the face of the other person, so as not to be caught staring. This was his answer: 'I don't think anything could be further from the truth. I certainly want to see socialism, but we're not going to create it by industrial chaos or by a workers' or peasants' revolt, but by the pressure we can exert on political parties. Mind you, it might come because the reforms we are seeking will arouse the ire of the establishment – then you might have a right-wing coup that might be doomed to failure – and then have a Spanish situation over again. But having said that, it's not true that I'm wanting to use the trade-union movement for political ends.'

*'The Role of Militancy', *New Left Review*, 1967.
†Edward Morton, of Mather & Platt.

Scanlon remembers Spain. He said in the *New Left Review* interview that the Spanish civil war was 'the real driving force to militancy' in his life at the time. He repaired Spanish Government vehicles in Britain, and joined the Communist Party, where he remained for about twenty years, until he left it in the mid-1950s after 'numerous political differences'.

The remarks of the personnel director didn't worry him. I asked him how he felt about possible public reaction to the aggressive pursuit of the workers' interests. 'In doing one's job one doesn't shrink from it because there might be some nasty aftermath,' he said. 'But to portray this as means to an end, to hope that socialism will come out of chaos, is the most reactionary political thing I can think of.'

Alarmists (who say they are not alarmists, merely realists) cite evidence of less orthodox forces at work. During the miners' strike of 1972, when Lord Wilberforce's court of inquiry, was hurriedly considering the evidence it had taken in public, there was an attempt by the authorities to drop a word into the ear of its members. It would be improper for such a court to listen to private solicitations, and there is no suggestion that this happened; no doubt the approach came in some innocuous guise, and was rejected as soon as it was identified. But the Government, or some of its members, certainly wanted to ensure that the miners received a substantial award. The story circulating in private was that 'King Street' had decided the miners wouldn't end the strike unless they were given 25 per cent. King Street means the headquarters of the Communist Party. The miners' union would deride any suggestion that the Communists controlled the course of the strike. The miners went back (for less than 25 per cent) when they thought they had squeezed the Government dry. But the story circulates in the shadows.

Trade-union militancy this century rose to its first peak before the First World War, to its second immediately afterwards. The number of working days lost in 1921 was nearly 86 million, far above anything in recent years. Most of these were in a single industry, coal mining. The figure for other industries was 13 million in 1921 and 18 million the year after; this compares with 13.5 million in 1971, the highest since the general strike of 1926 (1972 will be higher still). By the 1970s, strikes were comparatively peaceful affairs, though not as peaceful as people had grown accustomed to. Fifty and sixty years ago there was no shortage of violence, as trade unionists confronted the authorities.

Going back further again, into the nineteenth century, the early unions had leaned towards cooperation with employers. The boilermakers sang a jolly song in the 1870s:

> Capital and Labour seem
> By our Maker joined;
> Are they not like giant twins
> In the world of mind?

The boilermakers concluded it was just and meet

> Labour should cooperate
> And to help with all their might
> Masters to compete.

By 1889 Ben Tillett had formed his dockers' union (the cornerstone of today's T G W U) and in that year helped to bring the London dockers out in the most notable strike of the century. Labour was ceasing to cooperate. Twenty years later, at the end of Edwardian England, Tillett was a gifted mob orator who alarmed the upper classes, preaching revolution via industrial action, and leading dock strikes in 1911 and 1912. Miners and railwaymen were out in hundreds of thousands. On an August Sunday in Liverpool in 1911, hundreds were wounded and two killed in encounters with troops and police; a constable was kicked to death. Trains and signal boxes were attacked. In the same year ten people were killed in Llanelli after a weekend of bayonet charges and looting. *The Times* reported (January 1912) that Sir Joseph Compton-Rickett M.P. had told his constituents he was 'a constant and convinced supporter of trade unionism' but added that 'sooner than submit to anarchy the nation would temporarily accept a curtailment of liberty as the least of the two evils'. Sir Joseph ended with some pointed remarks about the awful prospect of unorganized masses in conflict with 'deadly modern weapons'. Spokesmen for both sides were more explicit in those days. Ben Tillett's annual report to his union for 1912 declared:

The lesson is that, in future strikes, the strikers must protest against the use of arms with arms; protest against shooting, with shooting; protest against violence, with violence . . . Capitalism is capitalism as a tiger is a tiger; and both are savage and pitiless towards the weak.*

In 1913 the unions had only four million members, less than a quarter of the country's workers.

The war cooled the situation, but it all began again after 1918. 'Direct action' sought to use strikes to force the Government to change the social order, via nationalization, workers' control of industry and a levelling of wealth; the left wing of unions and Labour Party embraced the slogan without being entirely clear about the consequences for parliamentary democracy. The general strike (162 million working days lost) was the muddled culmination of the workers' revolt; the unions, defeated as militants, settled down to a decade and a half of negotiation (and mass unemployment) until the next war started.

Egalitarian tendencies after 1945 were not, at first, reflected in the way the unions behaved. A Labour Government was in power, nationalizing industries and, hopefully, changing society at last. Strikes, forbidden during the war, remained theoretically illegal for several years after it. Most unions cooperated with the authorities, frowning on large wage demands by members, emerging as solidly respectable, responsible bodies that leader-writers could say kind things about. Arthur Deakin, the red-faced hammer of the Communists, was in command at the TGWU. Will Lawther at the miners believed that unofficial strikes were 'sheer treason'. Tom (later Lord) Williamson ran the General and Municipal Workers' Union with propriety. All are the type of union leader that Governments have in mind today when they talk of 'responsible' leadership. Deakin is dead, the other two retired. The moderate Lord Carron, who headed the engineers, was replaced by Scanlon in 1967. Scanlon had been biding his time in Manchester. He saw no virtue in being too

*This is not the language of the 1970s, despite the new militancy. An ex-member of the press department at the TGWU says that 'we used to play a game in here, putting the word "capitalist" in press releases. It was always knocked out by somebody higher up. It became "backward employer".'

respectable. As he remarked on television once: 'I say a little prayer every night which says, "Preserve me from becoming a respectable trade union official," because I know that when the other side are praising you, you're not necessarily doing your job.'*

Restraint began to crumble in the 1950s. By the end of the decade the postwar pattern had been set: hard bargaining by the unions, a growing number of strikes – mainly unofficial – and an uneasy sense of disorder in labour relations. The 1960s confirmed these developments. The unions spoke more harshly, and some of them threw up more radical leaders. The T G W U moved abruptly to the left when Deakin was replaced as general secretary by Frank Cousins, and continued in the same direction under Jack Jones after 1969. Lawrence Daly, a socialist who sees strikes as political weapons, became the miners' general secretary in 1968. Scanlon seized the presidency of the engineers from under the noses of the right-wing, who had a candidate ready to succeed Lord Carron. These union leaders, and others like them, were not much worried when Governments, the middle classes and Fleet Street criticized labour relations. They saw virtues in a militant membership that sent pay claims and waves of discontent surging up from below. What appeared to the critics as a lack of discipline could look like healthy democracy from inside the unions. Unions were not transformed. They went on being bureaucracies, generally cautious and conservative. But they were all affected, some willingly and some unwillingly, by the changes.

The question arose of what a union *was:* a hierarchy like a commercial firm, with bosses at the top and underlings who obeyed, or a looser structure in which power seeped upwards from the rank and file? The question contained the seeds of future trouble. It raised the matter of shop stewards: local leaders in the factories, elected by, and remaining among, the men they worked with – in one sense officials of the union, but in another, popular spokesmen who were free to act in what they regarded as the best interests of the local situation. If, at any time, certain acts by unions were to be made illegal, would they be held responsible for illegal behaviour by shop stewards? In 1972 the

*'Panorama', BBC TV, 1 May 1972.

answer (under the Industrial Relations Act) appeared to be Yes. This was very unwelcome to militant unions.

In the existing situation, shop stewards have little legal basis for their powers. Union rule books rarely mention them. Apart from two industries, coal mining and printing – where the formal union structure extends into the daily working life of pit and composing room, making shop stewards unnecessary – the stewards are the point of contact between union and members. The relationship is ill-defined; convenient for those who can exploit it without being held accountable.

From the 1950s, shop stewards were often in the news, especially if they could be called 'militant'. The shop stewards' movement had waxed and waned since it began during the First World War. Now it had emerged as an integral part of the system, with perhaps 175,000 representatives throughout industry. Their part was recognized by the Donovan Report of 1968,* which summed up its findings in the much-quoted epithet: 'Britain has two systems of industrial relations.' Donovan spelt out the tensions that arose between the formal system of industry-wide agreements and the informal system of factory bargaining. With full employment and labour always in demand, it suited managements and unions to bargain locally for piecework and overtime payments. This meant that basic earnings, agreed nationally, might bear little relationship to what men were actually paid. Among other things, said Donovan, the system led to local unofficial strikes. The solution offered by the Royal Commission was to accept the inevitable – local bargaining – but seek means of making it more orderly and less prone to strikes.

The Donovan Report identified defects in the bargaining system; others found defects in the unions and their relationship with the rest of the country. Andrew Shonfield, the economist and journalist, was a member of the commission. He wrote a 'note of reservation' which complained that the report 'barely

*Royal Commission on Trade Unions and Employers' Associations, 1965–8, under the chairmanship of Lord Donovan. It was the fifth Royal Commission into industrial relations in the last hundred years and the first since 1903. A Labour Government, prodded by the Conservatives, set it up.

concerns itself with the long-term problem of accommodating bodies with the kind of concentrated power which is possessed by trade unions to the changing future needs of an advanced industrial society'. He argued for more control over unions, whose powers grew as everyday life became more complex and dependent on interlocked services. Ten years earlier a group of anonymous Conservative lawyers, writing in the aftermath of the first real wave of industrial unrest since the war, had argued more sternly for curbing trade union powers. They proposed that 'political' strikes be forbidden and legal protection removed from those who struck without union agreement. One of the group was Sir John Donaldson, later the first president of the National Industrial Relations Court. Their booklet 'A Giant's Strength'* referred throughout to 'workmen', a word that smacks of the masters-and-men era, rather than the blander 'workers'. Shop stewards quickly saw it as a threat to their freedom as leaders of unofficial strikes. Unions were right to think it meant trouble. It was one of the planks from which the Conservative Party later built the Industrial Relations Act.

The Tory lawyers detected the mood of the militant trade unionists, in those days less powerfully placed. They found it dangerous, and they, too, were correct in what they observed. What they didn't foresee was how militancy would become central to the unions. The size of wage claims was to offer the clearest evidence. The pressure for more money grew through the 1960s. The Labour Government tried to freeze wages and prices in 1966; then the upward march continued. It was the militancy of men who always seemed to want more. The average earnings of manual workers were £16 a week in 1962, £28 in 1970. Inflation marched upwards, too. Retail prices at the end of 1970 were nearly half as much again as they had been in 1962. The average worker was better off in real terms, but nothing like as better off as the weight of his pay packet suggested.

The connection between wages and prices is involved; it

*The title is from Shakespeare's *Measure for Measure*:

> 'O it is excellent
> To have a giant's strength; but it is tyrannous
> To use it as a giant.'

confuses economists as well. The unions can be blamed largely or hardly at all for inflation, depending on one's point of view. But it is unarguable that wages and prices both increased at gathering speed. After price rises that averaged 3½ per cent a year in the early 1960s, the rate was 5 per cent in 1969, 8 per cent in 1970 and 9 per cent in 1971. By the end of that year, average earnings were £30 a week, and the Government was busy trying to hold down wage increases to a modest level in the large areas of the economy – the nationalized industries – where its influence was most direct.

At the same time, the Industrial Relations Act, designed to bring unions inside a formal legal framework, had been recognized by the unions as encroaching on their powers. In 1969 the unions had succeeded in forcing the Labour Government to emasculate its post-Donovan proposals, hopefully entitled 'In Place of Strife'; this proved the point about their strength that was causing alarm in the first place. The Conservative proposals went further and passed into law. What has given 1972 its special character was the way demands for improved wages and conditions, and the clamour against the Act, fused into a noisy expression of the union point of view. On the surface it showed the unions at their most militant for fifty years. The question that no one has cared to answer (or even to ask very often) is the extent to which this mood is not an aberration to be cured before society can proceed on its peaceful way, but something deep and lasting in trade-union thinking that seeks ends which must inevitably divert society into other ways. Many militants genuinely believe the Act is unfair because it stops them using their strength in the way they feel justified. Many workers feel they honestly deserve those increases in wages that make politicians wince.

It has been said that the demand for equality is the central dynamic of modern life. Trade unions are in the queue. They are members of a greedy society that perpetually rattles the rewards of affluence in everyone's face. It's hardly surprising that a more emancipated work-force, better informed about the world's goodies and who has most of them, should demand its share without wanting to be bothered by warnings of inflation.

'What people speak now is the language of expectations,' says an official at the T G W U. 'You've got a right to earn, let's say, £40 a week. You don't need to feel guilty about it.' If this is the key to the new militancy of the unions, the business of striking a fresh balance between governments and unions is going to be long and painful.

There is nothing new about industrial confrontation in Britain. At various times in the past, attitudes have hardened, grave accusations have been made; the worst has been expected, but it has never happened. The workers' demands and the authorities' concessions have always reached equilibrium. In his biography of Ernest Bevin (1960) Alan Bullock writes that

some of the charges levelled against the trade unions today might make more impression on them if they had not been heard so often before, at times when the unions had every justification for fighting in defence of their members' interests, and when their struggle to limit the arbitrary power of the employers and raise the status of the working class produced an expansion, not a restriction, of freedom.

No doubt a new equilibrium will be reached. But the present temper of the unions will need to be included in the calculation.

*

Militant unionists often seem a bloody-minded lot. When dockers ignored the National Industrial Relations Court and continued to picket the Midland Cold Store in east London in July 1972, insisting that the work should be theirs, five of them were gaoled for five days. They were picketing because their jobs are disappearing. That explained their behaviour without making it any more attractive. Dockers look aggressive and self-centred. They are frequently feared and disliked by fellow workers. During the cold-store dispute I met some of the counter-pickets, members of U S D A W, the Union of Shop, Distributive and Allied Workers, who were doing the jobs the dockers wanted. One man with shoulder-length hair looked furious when I suggested that dockers had problems. 'Afraid of losing work?' he said. '*Work?* Don't make me laugh. It's like Butlin's on the docks. They've got away with it for a long time, but they're not going to fucking get away with it here.'

The picture of dockers as grasping bullies was naturally the one that appealed to their critics. On the day the five dockers were released from gaol, the Prime Minister spoke on television about the pickets which were causing Midland Cold Store to lose £2,000 a week and driving it into bankruptcy. It was not fair, he said – the weak against the strong.* A few days later news leaked out that the brave little Midland Cold Store was an offshoot of one of the country's biggest conglomerates, the Vestey group. This had been closing down riverside facilities, where dockers worked, at the same time as it opened the Midland store with its identity concealed under a nominee. The news was excavated by The *Sunday Times*, having been first published by the small-circulation Marxist weekly, *Socialist Worker*. But the picketing dockers had suspected it all along. Lord Vestey, the exceedingly rich controller of Union International, was having rude things said about him on the docks long before the nation, including Edward Heath, knew the background. An old docker spoke in a radio programme a few days later, fumbling for words to make people understand. 'Life is a tug of war', he said. 'Lord Vestey owns half the world.'†

Those who aren't interested in making allowances for the unions see only the aggressiveness. The unions themselves are not overburdened with social conscience. They are in business to get what they can for their members. Stronger unions do better than weaker unions. As Harold Lever, the wealthy Labour M.P., has remarked,‡ few coal miners believe there's a moral law that says a High Court judge should earn five times as much as they do. Nor is there a moral law to say that newspaper printers (for instance) should earn twice as much as agricultural workers – well over £40 a week, against the farm-hands' £21. Printers have always been an élite, regarding themselves in the nineteenth century as the aristocracy of the working classes. With dockers and car workers, they are among the best-paid manual workers.

*'And what we were saying was, the weak – in other words fifty-seven men from USDAW, and the firm itself – ought to be able to get a fair deal against the strong who are bullying them.' From an interview in ITN's 'News at Ten', 26 July 1972.

†'It's Your Line', BBC Radio 4, 1 August 1972.

‡The *Observer*, 30 July 1972.

The sub-category of Fleet Street printers is especially favoured. They can interfere with production of a perishable product, in a section of the industry that works on modest margins. Fleet Street managements fear strikes, or the traditional device of the 'chapel' (branch) meeting in the middle of an evening, which stops production with the paper half-made. Printers on national newspapers earn an average of £69 a week, more than £3,500 a year.

John Bonfield, general secretary of the main printing union, the National Graphical Association, says that to talk of printers intimidating newspapers is exaggerated: the work is highly skilled, with great effort demanded at press time – 'the lads are entitled to a good wage'. He adds: 'Let's be frank about it, we are obviously in a strong bargaining position. What does one do about it? One bargains strongly. Short of instituting the kingdom of heaven on earth, those who are in the best bargaining position will do best. Could I as general secretary say, "You are in the best position, but don't use it"?' Well, no.

The middle classes have been worrying about the unions for a long time. A local dignitary in George Eliot's novel *Felix Holt the Radical*, set in the 1830s, complains that the Radicals 'want us to be governed by delegates from the trades-unions, who are to dictate to everybody, and make everything square to their mastery'. What troubles today's middle-class dreams is the new arrogance in the demeanour of the man who used to wear a cloth cap but now doesn't even have that badge of his humble station. One of the significant defeats for the Government in contesting wage claims involved the dustmen and other local government manual workers in 1970. In the unions' calendar of honour, it was part of 'the revolt of the low-paid workers'. A series of selective strikes organized by the unions involved was surprisingly effective. The episode, one felt, was a nasty jolt for suburban householders, brought face to face with accumulated rubbish and the knowledge that those men in gym shoes and thick gloves, brushing against your car and leaving a little trail of eggshells and polythene down the drive, could cause Governments to bend. An official of N U P E, the National Union of Public Employees (370,000 members; sixth largest) says there was some conscious psychology in planning the strike so that the public would be forcibly reminded of things they preferred to ignore. People, he pointed out sternly, don't want to know about hospital porters having to take arms and legs from operating theatres to the furnaces, or crematoria workers having to put burnt bones into grinding machines, or gravediggers, or what it's like down the sewers; the strike made them aware of dirt below the surface. There was a note of hysteria in correspondence to *The Times*. The main dispute had been settled to the dustmen's satisfaction, but Kensington and Chelsea Borough Council refused to pay the sums demanded for clearing up the backlog. Rubbish rotted in a thousand streets, infuriating residents.

Long after the strike, I went to meet a couple of the men who had been among the leaders in Kensington, Mr Sweeney and Mr Kearney. The council depot was in a grimy corner of Ladbroke Grove, where a motorway on stilts is the only sign of progress; one of London's backyards. We sat in a bare room, the door locked, for some reason, around a heavy table with legs like twisted treacle that must once have stood in a family dining-room. Sweeney wore a check beret with a bobble and a red shirt under a blue linen jacket; he had a droopy moustache. Kearney, a big Irishman, sat up straight in a well-cut suit, and said he was a bingo-caller in his spare time.

'There were working-class people lived in all those little turnings when I was a kid,' observed Sweeney. 'Now they're paying forty thousand and forty-five thousand pounds for the houses, so they can have cocktail parties in 'em with the Archbishop of Somewhere saying, "Oh, Sir Malby, what about my dustbin"?'

Sir Malby Crofton, leader of the Conservative majority on Kensington and Chelsea Council, kept coming up in conversation. Sir Malby wrote more than one letter to *The Times* after the strike. 'Have we gone mad in this country?' he asked. 'Can we no longer insist that men do a fair day's work for a fair day's pay?' He said that on top of the £26 or so a week the dustmen would be getting under the settlement, people gave them tips; he knew of a restaurant in the King's Road that paid a refuse gang a private £10 a week for its services. 'I would guess that some of our dustmen will be in the £2,000 a year class,' he wrote. Dustmen know where they stand with Sir Malby, who is a stockbroker.

Kearney said his average earnings were £27 a week, and 'if you get three or four bob a day in tips, it pays for your breakfast'. That was why he worked part-time as a bingo-caller, four nights a week. He liked the open-air life. He said that, believe it or not, 'I've had a head pop out and say "Would you like a cup of tea or a brandy, dustman?"' A *brandy*? 'Of course,' he said, 'I'm not talking of your rank Tories. I'm talking of the ordinary ratepayer who's satisfied with the way his bin has been left.' Sweeney was tapping his teeth gently with the corner of a packet of Players. 'That strike,' he said, grinning at me sideways, 'it was like a giant waking up from a long sleep, never to sleep again.' He seemed to be laughing at me and being serious at the same time. Kearney, without any prompting, said what the official at NUPE had said. 'Before the strike people never realized what the sewers were for. They pull the chain and think, that's it. It's not.'

At about the time Sweeney and Kearney were talking to me, union officials were busy preparing a dustman's-and-sewerman's wage claim for the autumn of 1972. It was rather bigger than the one that caused the strike two years earlier.

'The lads had some lovely rubbish to dump outside Sir Malby's house,' said Sweeney, happily. 'But they had four policemen there all the time. A few 999 calls got rid of three of them, the other one was two hundred yards away, and they dumped it.' It was an episode that led to more acrimonious letters in *The Times*. 'I have no evidence that this was a protest gesture,' wrote Sir Malby, 'but there must at least be a strong presumption that it was.'

Before I left, Sweeney drew my attention to an embroidered ecclesiastical vestment hanging spread out on the wall, and said he bet I didn't expect to see anything like that. There was a booklet on the table about the example of Soviet Russia. As he unlocked the door, Kearney said I mustn't think that the lads were at odds with the council. 'We've got good relations,' he said. 'But we haven't bowed down.' Sweeney just smiled.

2. The Greedy Society

Sixty years ago, in May 1912, when the country was torn with labour unrest, a young Member of Parliament, Eliot Crawshay-Williams, remarked in the House of Commons that one reason the workers were in revolt was that 'during the last ten years, riches have exhibited themselves more flamboyantly than ever before, partly through the motor car'. It was a wise observation. Crawshay-Williams recognized 'the feeling on the part of labour that it is not getting its fair share of the world's goods. The balance is on the wrong side, and the worker, who is better educated than his ancestors, is well aware of it.'

It could have been yesterday. So could Crawshay-Williams's bafflement, which came later in the speech, about 'the rise in the price of living, due to increased wages being met by an increase in the price of the product for which those increased wages were paid'. It was a conundrum, later to be solved, in terms of 1912 standards of living, partly by a modest redistribution of wealth, largely by increases in the amount of wealth being distributed. But the solution was only relative. Sixty years later, the improvement in real earnings has not taken the edge off appetites, or removed the feeling that the workers were failing to get their share. The clamour for more money is just as loud and more sophisticated. The arguments about wages pushing up prices pushing up wages have continued to be as relevant, or irrelevant, as they were in that far-off country of farthings and sovereigns.

It would have dismayed the liberals of 1912, who would presumably have thought that earnings of two and three times as much, once the economic or social miracle of providing them had been performed, might have been expected to please the hottest militant. Wage and cost-of-living comparisons are notoriously difficult, but the general picture is clear enough.

Railway locomotive drivers earned about £120 a year in 1912 and about £1,800 a year in 1972. The cost of living rose roughly eight times over that period, making drivers twice as well off in real terms. This seems to be true of most skilled workers. The unskilled have done better still. Farm hands averaged less than £50 a year before the First World War, and by 1972 had reached £1,100, or three times as much in real terms. Railway porters, £50-a-year men in 1912, now average £1,500 and are nearly four times better off.

What changed were people's expectations. The material world opened up, technology produced its marvels, mass advertising told everyone what to covet, films and then television made others' possessions that much more tangible and desirable. The question of what constituted 'a fair share' became more intractable, as it came to be asked in terms, not of bare subsistence but of butter instead of margarine or cars instead of bicycles. It was always an awkward question to decide what a man 'ought' to earn. In another Parliamentary debate of 1912 – a year, like 1972, that made many look uneasily under the surface of life in Britain – Lord Cecil expressed sympathy with the workers but pointed out that they, like the rest of the competitive world, had to take their chance in the market. 'We always try to get whatever we want as cheaply as we can,' he said, 'and when Hon. members say that the labourer ought to get so much for his work, the true answer is that it is not a question of "ought" at all... It is no more reasonable to say that they ought to have such a rate of wage than to say that a person ought to be able to buy cheaper at one shop or sell dearer at another.'

Marx said the unions should stop talking about 'a fair day's work for a fair day's pay', and demand the overthrow of the wages system altogether. But there was a shortage of revolutionaries; the wages system survived, and so did the 'fair deal' notion, which suited many people, especially employers, by giving the system an air of propriety. As though by magic, society had always known that dockers should earn more than farm labourers, and bishops should earn more than both of them put together. What seems to have been happening since the 1950s is that numbers of people – rather than handfuls of theoreticians – have begun to challenge these assumptions. Affluent, on the whole, by the standards of the past, they would like to be more affluent still. If they are willing to use the language of 'a fair deal', of what it is 'reasonable' to ask, they interpret it as meaning fair and reasonable in the light of their expectations. But they tend not to use these terms. The phrase, 'a fair day's work for a fair day's pay', which used to appear in a TGWU booklet about bargaining, has now been removed. Clive Jenkins, who leads the white-collar wing of the unions with fierce Welsh dedication, summed up his approach in a leaflet issued some years ago by ASSET, his former union. He wrote:

REMEMBER, collective bargaining in Britain is myth-ridden. It is saddled with such shabby worn-out folk tales as 'a fair day's pay for a fair day's work'. This is nonsense – particularly for supervisors and technicians. All wages and salaries demonstrate a direct relationship to leverage. The more strongly organized an occupation becomes, the higher its rewards.

What it is practical to obtain is more important than what a worker is entitled to, since who in our society is in a position to lay down the law about anyone's entitlement? The worker is entitled to a lot more – it seems this is as far as the argument need be taken. Riches exhibit themselves as flamboyantly as ever. It's true that some wealth has been taken from the top and spread more thinly lower down. Before 1914 the top one per cent of the adult population owned 69 per cent of total personal wealth by 1968 the same proportion of people owned only 33 per cent. The top tenth of the nation owned 92 per cent of personal wealth before 1914, but this has now fallen to 75 per cent. A rich man's income, in 1912, was lightly taxed. The publishing empire of Lord Northcliffe gave him a personal cash-flow of £150,000 a year or more, equivalent to well over a million pounds today.*

*In the year ending 31 March 1903 he earned £146,691, mainly from investments in his own publications, and got through £94,753 of it. Items include: running three houses, £20,699; allowances to relatives, £25,909; presents and gifts, £10,113; personal spending for himself and his wife, £13,050; motorcar expenses, £6,276; stables, wine, tobacco and telephone, £2,598; charities and donations, £6,369; travelling and hotels, £5,418; fishing expenses, £396. Multiply by eight for 1972 equivalents.

It meant that he was earning three thousand times as much as a labourer. To provide a similar rich/poor differential today would mean an income clear of tax of around £3 million, virtually impossible with taxation at its present levels; and there were many Northcliffes before 1914. But capital gains in a period of intense inflation can provide equally spectacular results. Stock-exchange flotations produce a steady flow of millionaires, and so does property dealing and speculation. The difference is that before 1914 the rich were more or less left alone to get on with becoming richer. They were attacked in scurrilous publications by hot-headed revolutionaries, but the voice of society spoke approvingly, because to all intents and purposes, they *were* society.

Today the rich and their riches are viewed more objectively. There is much ambivalence about this. To the radical observer, Fleet Street and television are still part of a conspiracy to maintain privilege. But it's a half-hearted conspiracy. *The Times* recently printed two articles on the same page.* One was in the form of an open letter to Edward Heath and his ministers, from an anonymous company director who had lost his job and come down in the world, where he had met the working class for the first time. 'To them,' he wrote, 'you are a plummy-voiced, granite-hearted lot of bastards who are out to kill the unions and grind them down. And everything you say about inflated wage demands confirms it.' The other was an article by Bernard Levin, not usually the unions' best friend, who wrote about the current railwaymen's demands and asked Heath a number of pertinent questions. 'Has he any idea what a man earning £20 a week feels,' he wrote, 'when he sees speculators about to make untold millions by befouling Piccadilly Circus and Covent Garden and indeed any other bits of any other city that they can get their hands on?'

It would be remarkable if the unions didn't seek to advance their interests, egged on by their old sense of grievance, and their new sense of egalitarianism or pride or arrogance or whatever word one uses to describe the shift in social attitudes that has come about in the last quarter of a century. Groups of workers have gambled on their strength and been successful – not always,

*30 May 1972.

but often enough to set the tone. The miners went on strike early in 1972 with a claim that the Government refused to consider. In the previous two years they had received increases worth 20 per cent overall. When they emerged victorious from the strike, they had won a further 21 per cent.

Professional workers usually move more stealthily, but just as effectively. In the early 1960s, many doctors became aware (like the miners, ten years later) that they had slipped badly in relation to other trades and professions. Consultants were doing well; junior hospital doctors were doing badly, but they carried no political weight; it was the general practitioners who were both underpaid (in their own estimation) and in a position to wreck the Health Service if they weren't properly rewarded. In 1963 the average G. P. earned £4,200 gross* from the NHS. In 1914 terms, he was roughly twice as well off (though increased taxation would reduce the margin). Much hard bargaining was led by the British Medical Association – the GPs' principal professional body, which is dismayed to be regarded as a trade union, but acts uncommonly like one when it's so inclined. The result was that by 1971 the average G. P.'s gross earnings were £7,400. This was an increase of 75 per cent. In the same period the cost of living rose 55 per cent. The doctors were winning.

Overall, the wage increases that are now causing so much alarm reached what the Government regarded as a danger level in 1970, when average weekly earnings of manual workers rose by 13.7 per cent. People began to talk about the 'wages explosion'. Edward Heath, then leader of the Opposition, said just before the General Election in June 1970 that 'the wage explosion is the way in which, when all else fails, those who are able to do so protect their living standards'; a more benign view than he took when he became Prime Minister. In 1971 earnings were up 10.1 per cent, and the 1972 figure looks like being higher. It was not the picture of former years. In the early 1960s, 4 and 5 per cents were the order. In Mordecai Richler's novel *Cocksure* (1968), a visiting American reads that the postmen

---

*Practice expenses must be paid from gross earnings. But G.P.s are able to blur the distinction between 'personal' and 'practice' expenditure, and so obtain tax relief on a larger slice of their personal income.

are striking for another fifteen shillings. 'Two dollars', he thinks. 'Well, that wasn't exactly peanuts, maybe they would settle for half.' Then he looks at the newspaper again. 'No, no, they weren't asking for another two dollars an hour. Incredibly enough, what they seemed to want was two dollars more a week.' He thinks it must be a misprint, and so it would be nowadays. No one wastes time asking for an increase of 75p a week; the scale of things has changed. Various explanations have been put forward for this new aggressiveness. The Labour Government's wage-and-price freeze in 1966 could be expected to lead to a surge of demand as soon as it was broken. The devaluation of the pound in November 1967 raised import prices and so increased the cost of living; so did the higher consumer taxes that followed devaluation. The intention was to reduce consumption in Britain so that more goods would be exported and the balance of payments improved. But the workers whose consumption should have been reduced retaliated by asking for more money to go on living as they had been accustomed to : unsettling for the economy but not altogether surprising.

Another suggested factor is that success in pushing up earnings 'may have given individual trade unions an unexpected glimpse into the very large monopolistic powers which they possess for pushing money wage rates up and which they have not fully exploited in the past'.* But the 'monopolistic powers' of unions had been unchanged for years, and had been used to the full in previous encounters. The feeling one gets is not of a new version of the trade-union machine, but of fresh steam getting into the cylinders of the old one.

The kindly Welfare State, cushioning workers against unemployment and strikes, has been cited as another factor in their ready militancy. Social security benefits are paid to the wives and children of men on strike. A new Act in 1971 reduced the amount payable when other income (such as strike pay) was being received. But benefits continue to give basic protection.† A family

*Professor James E. Meade of Cambridge University in the Wincott Memorial Lecture, September 1971.

†Leaflets handed out during strikes claim that 'Social Security is the biggest strike fund of all.' An organization called the Claimant and

with two children might be drawing eight or nine pounds a week, plus rent, rates and school fares. In theory strike pay is not worth giving a family man, since payment of, say, £5 a week will reduce social security benefit by £4. In practice it doesn't always work out like that; some strikers manage to slide past the regulations, and draw their money both ways. One union which frequently has small local strikes to deal with is said to have developed a system of pretending to give no strike pay, but handing out a lump sum on some pretext when the strike is over. The other (legal) source of income for strikers is in refunds of income tax, which become payable at once.*

None of these explanations of why unions are more militant seems satisfactory, though all probably contribute. It is the underlying mood that is crucial. The part played by advertising in encouraging consumer appetites would be worth studying. In one of the few comments on this aspect, Malcolm Crawford wrote in The *Sunday Times*:†

Real demands seem to have become higher and more insistent. Were workers really content with less in [the 1960s]? Possibly so. A car – which is not only expensive, but is a source of continuing expense – is now regarded as a necessity, whereas it generally was not in the mid-1950s. Television advertising may have raised the consumption threshold – not to mention the more systematic selling of material opulence just outside your reach, in the glossy magazines.

Percentage increases in spending in real terms (with figures adjusted to offset inflation) show that between 1960 and 1965, spending on cars and motor bikes rose on average 7.4 per cent each year. From 1965 to 1970 the increase was 3.6 per cent, only to shoot up to 26.3 per cent in 1971. Radio and electrical goods and alcoholic drink showed large increases in 1971. Spending on food, which had risen by a steady one per cent each

Unemployed Workers' Union, run from Barnsley by an ex-miner, Joe Kenyon, fights cases and issues literature. 'So let's all become MILITANT OLIVERS and ask for more,' writes Kenyon.

*The amount depends on how much tax has already been paid. A married man with two small children, earning £30 a week, who went on strike in October, halfway through the financial year, would receive £7 a week for about eight weeks.

†23 April 1972.

year since 1960, dropped for the first time in 1971, by 0.3 per cent. Some, clearly, couldn't afford quite so much. Others could, and put their money into whisky, cars and tape recorders.

One argument for restraint that might appeal to the unions, not out of charity but in their own interest, is that by raising wages they cause inflation and so defeat their own ends as well as everyone else's. It does not appeal to them, although to many people, and most of the media, it is the central issue. Leading articles on the subject assume as a matter of course that rising prices are caused by rising wages. The unions say it's the other way round, the demand for wages arising because of inflation produced by Government policies. 'Organized labour is being made the scapegoat for inflation,' Jack Jones told the Labour Party conference in 1970. 'The Goebbels big-lie technique is being practised.' The Trades Union Congress, the soft centre of the trade union organization, calculated that in the two years 1967–9, when retail prices rose by 11 per cent, wages contributed only 3 or 4 per cent, the remainder coming from import costs after devaluation (3 per cent), indirect taxes (4 per cent) and capital costs (1 per cent). These figures have been disputed; in any case, even left-wing economists concede that, since 1969, wage increases have been a larger element in inflation. But precisely how the two interact is beyond objective analysis.

The retail price index rose by nearly 10 per cent in 1971. This was the figure that brought the groundswell of panic, with the *Economist* pointing out that 10 per cent annually at compound interest meant that prices would double every seven years. At the end of a working lifetime of fifty years, a wage-earner's original pound would be worth less than one new penny at the former value. A gin and tonic fifty years hence would cost £32; a modest family car £120,000; a four-bedroomed house in the suburbs not less than £1,500,000. The increase slowed in the first part of 1972; most commentators said this wouldn't last.

The unions stolidly blamed inflation for driving them to seek higher wages. Or they pointed to the plight of low-paid workers. Just as 'average earnings' conceal the substantially higher wages of a small number of dockers and car workers, so they conceal the much lower earnings of others. The official Family

Expenditure Survey for 1969 (when average earnings were £25) showed that a quarter of male manual workers earned less than £18.75 a week.

The trouble with selective increases for those at the bottom of the heap is that few workers higher up will tolerate a narrowing gap. They want increases, too; they have their status to think of. A rise for poor Joe becomes a rise for all the other Joes. There is a powerful moral case for levelling incomes in society. There is also a case for doing it inside unions.

The amount of overtime further complicates the low-earnings picture. Millions habitually work overtime, so that 'average earnings' reflect the equivalent of an extra five or six hours' work a week. About a third (1.6 million) of the operatives in manufacturing industry work a weekly average of eight hours overtime. Is the man who would be poorly paid if he didn't work overtime entitled to claim that he is poorly paid in any case, since overtime is an optional extra that deprives him of leisure?

Much has been written about the 'poverty trap', the factor that makes those with low earnings especially vulnerable to income tax. This is because the threshold at which tax becomes payable has fallen; so that when gross earnings increase, they are bitten into first by tax on the total amount, then by inflation on what's left. This can happen to earnings at any level, but its effects on those of £20 to £30 a week are disproportionately harsh. Allied with the 'poverty trap' is the argument that to measure pay increase as percentages discriminates against those whose earnings are small to begin with. Fifteen per cent sounds a lot, but 15 per cent of what? If a man earning £25 a week gets a 20 per cent increase, it will be worth only £250 a year; a manager with a salary of £5,000 can have an acceptable rise of 7½ per cent and find himself £375 better off. The 'dockers' tanner', successfully fought for by Ben Tillett and John Burns in 1889, was a minimum of 6d. an hour for labourers instead of 5d.: an increase of 20 per cent. Dr Hilda Behrend of Edinburgh University says *

*In a symposium, 'Incomes policy in Britain: policy proposals and research needs', National Institute of Economic and Social Research, 1972. Here, and in other papers, Dr Behrend suggests that the word 'inflation' is meaningless to many people. In 1971 she found that 56 per cent of a sample

that many people fail to grasp how much, or how little, percentage increases mean to them in money. 'If they did,' she says, 'would the less well paid members of society acquiesce in a percentage norm which gives more extra money per week to the higher paid than to the lower paid? This makes one wonder whether the reason that the practice has not been queried more often in the past is that the people who understand the idea most readily are also those who gain most from its application.'

Few of these notions appeal to politicians who have the task of curbing inflation. They see it as a desperate matter, and no doubt it is. But numbers of trade unionists refuse to read the same message into the situation. They are beyond persuasion for the moment. When the Prime Minister says that unions must stop pursuing excessive wage claims, it becomes a matter of defining 'excessive'. When Sir Alec Douglas-Home tells his constituents that 'we must curb our greed if it is not to destroy us', he invites an obvious response from union journals like 'TASS News',* which mused on who was meant by 'us' – the Queen, Arnold Weinstock, David Frost, the Institute of Directors? – and rejected Sir Alec's views as 'based on selfishness and ignorance'. There seems little point in berating citizens of a frenetic consumer society because they earn thirty pounds a week and would like to earn forty.

One argument often heard is that at a time of rapidly rising wages and prices, the strong sweep ahead, leaving the weak gasping at the roadside: pensioners, retired gentlefolk with a few unenterprising investments, workers who are unable or unwilling to bargain as fiercely as the pace-setters. But since the competitive system has never been unduly worried about letting the strong grab what they can, it is hard to find moral grounds for interfering when groups of workers apply the same philosophy. They are selfish, of course. But then, who isn't? The only argument that matters is the unsentimental one that

---

didn't know what it meant; answers ranged from 'something to do with money' to 'blowing up a bicycle tyre'.

*TASS is the Technical and Supervisory Section of the AUEW. A militant white-collar group, it was formerly DATA, the Draughtsmen's and Allied Technicians' Association.

if wages rise faster than productivity, inflation grows. If trade unions refuse to accept the implications of this – suggesting, for instance, that company profits (up 17.7 per cent in the first half of 1972) should be reduced – then the opposing elephants meet with a hollow thud, and the strongest skull wins. It is laughable to think of a voluntary pay policy succeeding in this atmosphere.

For the moment the unions press on. A recent issue of a TGWU newspaper* pointed out with distaste that manual workers in the Scottish Borders area earned £7 a week less than the national average because of their unfortunate habit of loyalty to 'the maisters', an attitude that was 'the bane of all negotiations' in the local tweed and knitwear industries. 'The departure of the respectful forelock-tugging worker from the Borders scene cannot come too soon,' added the writer. J. E. Mortimer, a former union official who now works (at £10,000 a year) as a director of London Transport, says that 'they are like men with a different scale of appetites. I don't think trade union officials are any less idealistic. They haven't got a two-pork-chops mentality – to suggest that would be to slander them. But people are thinking in more ambitious terms. Not only about wages but about their right to work, and pensions, and holidays – there's a new dimension, a new scale of expectation.'

More ominously, the official at the TGWU said simply: 'We've got to teach the lads to ask for more. At the moment they're just nibbling.'

*The Highway, June 1972.

3. It's a Battlefield

The Industrial Society occupies a large house near Marble Arch, where it runs courses and conferences on management and industrial relations. Its aim is to 'promote the best use of people at work'. The hall has a signed photograph of the Duke of Edinburgh and a display stand with a pair of sombre neckties in navy and plum, as worn by managers. The society is independent and self-financing, and a quarter of its council members are trade-union officials. Specialist advisers visit companies and trade unions. It publishes filmstrips and booklets ('The Manager as a Leader'; 'Facilities for Shop Stewards'). It has an efficient information service. People who have heard of the society but who have not been there tend to be vague about what, exactly, it's for. A few weeks after I had been there twice, I found I couldn't quite remember; I had to re-read the literature to remind myself. It seems to be for better relations: for oiling the wheels with understanding. It isn't a battlefield inside the Industrial Society. The director, John Garnett, a big, jumpy man who used to be a manager with I C I, is esteemed in industrial relations circles; he talks passionately of 'winning the minds and hearts of men'.

I attended the first session of a three-day course for newcomers to personnel management. There were eighteen men and one girl: some were young trainees, others were foremen or managers, and older. We sat at desks placed in a horseshoe, with the course adviser at the open end, a woman wielding a black crayon, which she used on large sheets of paper pinned to a board and easel. The first thing she wrote was:

> MANAGEMENT:
> acquire – knowledge
> cultivate – patience
> achieve – understanding

Presently a new sheet was in use to show the five Ms:

Money Machines Materials Methods Men

The adviser said that men were the most important resource that industry possessed. She wrote it down. 'There's an awful lot of talk about troublemakers in industry,' she went on. 'But every troublemaker is somebody's employee, and if he's causing trouble, I put it down to management's fault. There must be something wrong. Since the war, we've been too apt to say it's the fault of the unions, but I put a lot of it down to the fault of managements.'

The adviser gave a sympathetic picture of the worker: his job was often boring, he resented high profits, managements could be remote, and between him and starvation he had nothing but a week's wages; no capital. Then she asked for comments. A stocky middle-aged man with glasses and a brown suit, described on the course list as a production executive, said abruptly: 'I think your lecture's twenty years out of date. The workers who work under me on the whole earn a damn sight more than I do – you say they've only got one week's wages between them and the workhouse, but it's a damn big wage.'

A couple of 'Hear hears' followed this. The adviser smiled, crayon at the ready. She continued to sound sympathetic to the workers, referring once to 'wage slaves', but changed gear when she came to the unions. Their role, everyone agreed, was to get the best deal for their members. The trouble was, said a manager, they took a short-term view. 'I'd agree with you here', said the adviser. 'The worker is concerned with the short-term, and so is the union. They don't say, "What good will this do the country?" What they think of today is, "What's in it for us?" But then, there are a lot of political motives behind what's happening today.'

This promising line wasn't pursued. We drifted through incentives and wage differentials to contemplate fitters earning £70 in one industry and £30 in another. There was a general murmuring against union selfishness. A coloured executive with an overseas company said that 'trade union leaders are in it for themselves', and the adviser nodded vigorously. 'You've hit the nail right on the head', she said. 'I'm very very pro-worker – but by that I also mean management, the whole lot. Trade unions are losing sight of their aims.'

Eventually the conversation came full circle, back to the workers and their individuality. It seemed to have been at two levels. On one of them, workers were ordinary chaps who needed only to be understood and consulted in order that they should give of their best. On the other, the unions could be awkward and selfish. The message seemed to be that people were reasonable, but their organizations could make them less so.

At a later session, near the end of the course, I sat in on a mock negotiation between shop stewards and managements, three a side. They argued about an afternoon tea-break, withdrawn because of abuse. The adviser cunningly picked a more senior manager, Jack, to play the leading steward, with a nervous young trainee, Philip, to head the company team. They sat on opposite sides of the table. 'The cost of your abusing this privilege is quite unacceptable to management,' said Philip. Jack looked at him stonily and said: 'You should have consulted me before putting up that notice. Conditions in that department are hot and stuffy, and in order to revive themselves they have to consume two cups of tea, which takes longer than ten minutes. I can confidently state that my brothers and sisters will not stand for the withdrawal of the tea break.'

Soon the management team was reduced to muttering incoherently about abuse. When Philip tried to instance delays on the production lines, Jack shook his head. 'That's a management problem. Those are management problems.' Predictably, the shop stewards won. Philip and colleagues made red-faced concessions. When the course were discussing it later, the coloured man got quite worked up. 'Your attitude was intolerable,' he said to Jack. Jack looked up from his Action Notes and Points for Communication. 'I've never met a shop steward whose attitude wasn't,' he said.

*

The real battlefield is well trampled; the best efforts of conciliatory men have a lot to cope with. The rest of this chapter traces the mood of some crucial wage settlements in the last two years. Murmurings among the low-paid had begun in 1969. That autumn, negotiators at the National Joint Council for Local Authorities' Service – where wages of dustmen, drivers and other town-hall workers are agreed – had reached deadlock over a laughable little increase of 75p a week. In any pay dispute affecting nationalized industries and local government, a defeat has special disadvantages for governments. It looks 'official', with the blessing, tacit or otherwise, of the authorities; it gets well publicized; and it is likely to affect hundred of thousands of workers at a time. Nearly half the country's trade unionists work in the public sector, from railways to the Health Service, and a much larger proportion are union members than in private industry. Local authorities employ more than 800,000 manual workers (two-thirds of them women cleaners and school-kitchen helps), all of whom stand to gain by industry-wide pay rises. When the 1969 negotiations failed, London dustmen began unofficial strikes; and against this background, the unions did better than usual.

A year later they were back for more, this time with plans for official, selective strikes by dustmen, sewage-plant workers, drivers, messengers and gravediggers. The claim was the usual complicated package covering allowances and supplements that no newspaper could ever print in full for fear of sending readers to sleep. The hard core was a request for £2.75 all round. Looking back on it, a N U P E official says that 'we had the wind under our tails, we were going for the jackpot. Whatever we'd been offered, we'd have gone for a bit more.' This hearty approach, which is what employers often suspect and unions usually deny, was strongly resisted.

After three weeks of strikes the claim went to an independent committee of inquiry under Sir Jack Scamp of G E C, an authority on industrial settlements, which recommended a £2.50 rise. Almost worse, the committee said in a voice of despair that since most of the year's pay settlements had been inflationary, there was small hope of arresting the trend with the dustmen. The arithmetic came out at around 15 per cent.

It was a bad season for inflation. Power-station men were soon asking for £5.80. When they failed to get it, they banned overtime shortly before Christmas, causing widespread power cuts. Another court of inquiry was summoned, this time under a High Court judge, Lord Wilberforce, and awarded the men increases of around two or three pounds, which they accepted. The package was so complicated that no one could be sure how much it was worth as a percentage. The Government said it was 10.9 per cent and a victory for restraint, the unions said it was 15.4 per cent and a victory for natural justice.

Either way the Government did noticeably better in 1971 with a 9½ per cent here (the railways) and an 8½ per cent there (the industrial civil service). Best of all from the point of view of encouraging the others, it defeated 210,000 Post Office postmen, clerks and telephonists after forty-seven days, the longest national strike in Britain since the war.*

The Union of Post Office Workers spent its reserves of £500,000 and borrowed £750,000 from other unions; a year later it was still in a state of shock. Tom Jackson, the general secretary, says now that they should have used different tactics. They should have been selective, pouncing on clerical services in one place and letter deliveries in another, at minimal cost to themselves. 'But the lads all wanted to come out at the same time and have that nice warm feeling,' he says. Having asked for 15 per cent and been offered eight, they were finally forced to accept nine, awarded them by another court of inquiry, which said it was not in the national interest to give them any more. One member of the three-man court, John Hughes,† dissented. He said that the national interest was outside the court's terms of reference, and suggested that the Post Office workers had been chosen as an object lesson in how to stop inflation. At an emotional conference the following year ('No Requiem – a Rebirth!'

*A longer company strike was going on at the same time, at the Ford Motor Co., whose 50,000 workers wanted a £15 increase. After nine weeks and much bitterness they got £8 spread over two years. Militants, of whom there were plenty, said it was a defeat.

†Hughes, an economist, is vice principal of Ruskin College – in Oxford, but not part of the university – and runs a Trade Union Research Unit there. This was set up in 1970, mainly with TGWU money, after Hughes had been to see Jack Jones. The unit has prepared a number of wily wage claims, including the TGWU's case to Ford that ended in the 1971 strike.

was the headline in the union newspaper), Jackson said of the inquiry: 'We have been cheated and robbed just as surely as if our pockets had been picked.'

A postman's average earnings after the increase were £29 a week. Like so many settlements, it meant what observers wanted it to mean. The employers were not oppressing the poor, as in the old days; perhaps they were oppressing the comparatively poor, but that didn't have the same ring. Many middle-class people (and affluent workers) can regard such a strike with split minds. There is sympathy for a case reasonably presented, with a personable leader like Jackson (bushy moustache, big friendly face) to appear on television. There is an uneasy feeling that those mild-mannered men who deliver letters, those bored-looking clerks behind post office counters, wouldn't be staying out week after week unless they had a sense of conviction. There is also a feeling that a man who will be earning £1,500 a year can't be too badly off. The fact that numbers of girl telephonists refused to join the strike was dwelt on by press and television. This is the attitude among journalists that militant trade unionists find unforgivable: they are fellow workers, yet they write articles praising scabs and making much of public inconvenience. But the journalist himself is often divided: sympathizing with the hard case, nervously apprehensive about inflation horror stories.

During 1971 many articles were written suggesting that the Conservative Government had at last come to grips with its pay policy. The teeth had begun to bite; the whip was cracking; the door was closing. In retrospect the metaphors provide an ironic prelude to the events of 1972 that blew in with the New Year. The teeth turned to rubber; the whip was a piece of string. The word 'confrontation' has been worked to death, but it was hard to resist using it about the ugly conflict between miners and Government. The National Union of Mineworkers, calling its first national stoppage since the General Strike of 1926, demonstrated the strength of the workers in a way that brought tears to the eyes of the left. By a combination of force and righteousness the miners made the authorities listen to their argument that they were a 'special case' whose earnings had lagged in comparison with those in other industries.

Miners were not particularly well paid for their labours, but nor were they particularly badly paid. What mattered was that they were able to present their situation as an outrage to natural justice, and have this publicly accepted by Wilberforce's court of inquiry. As well as the 'special case' of their place in the wage tables was the special case of their lives as miners. Eighty or ninety are killed each year; hundreds badly injured. But there is a case, if a milder one, to be made out in many industries. Why stop at miners? In the past they were the battering ram of the unions in attacking the system. Perhaps they still are. If it was impossible to deny justice to the miners, it might soon be impossible to deny it to others. In that case the miners' strike could be seen as a piece of revolutionary politics as well as an industrial dispute.

The odd thing about the strike was that few people, except presumably the miners, thought it would happen, or gave it much hope of success once it had begun. The general decline of coal mining since 1957, when demand for coal began to fall, has pushed it away from its central place. It is yesterday's industry. More than 700,000 miners worked at 950 collieries in 1947, when the Government took over coal 'on behalf of the people'. By 1971 there were 290 collieries and 287,000 men, though output per head had nearly doubled, mainly because of mechanization. The steady running down of the industry, and the National Coal Board's need to make coal as competitive as possible against other fuels, was the background against which the miners had negotiated – successfully, for a number of years. In 1967 their average earnings were £22.60 a week, compared with £21.13 in manufacturing industries. But over the next four years the miner's earnings rose to £28.10 and were overtaken by the factory worker's £30.20.

The circumstances were peculiar to mining. Both the union and the Coal Board had sought for years to do away with the piecework system and the complicated wages structure based on local rates, replacing them with fixed national earnings. From 1966 the policy was extended to cover subsequent wage increases. The earnings of men in highly-paid coalfields, such as Kent and Nottinghamshire, were held back so that the worse-paid areas like Scotland and Wales could catch up. This restraint told heavily in the miners' favour when their case was examined, as did the years of cooperation in running down coal mining. Unlike most industries they had actually helped the lower-paid; they had robbed Peter to pay Paul. The union argued that the men had done more than their share. It pointed out that the new fixed rates, desirable though they were in producing order out of chaos, gave little scope for pushing up earnings by local bargaining, as practised through much of industry.

When the arguments were marshalled for the inquiry – after six weeks of strike, massive power disconnections and a million and a half men laid off work – they were suddenly found to be lucid and penetrating; perhaps even more penetrating than they really were. But before the strike they meant nothing to the Coal Board. In 1969 the Board had given the union all it asked for, an increase worth about 7 per cent overall. Even so, unofficial strikes broke out over demands for a shorter week. By 1970 the NUM was doing its sums more carefully and raised its demands sharply. Failure to agree would have led to a strike then, but the miners' is one of the few unions that must ballot its members first. A two-thirds majority was needed, and only 55½ per cent voted in favour. Eventually the union settled for increases worth 12 per cent. In 1971 the miners' annual conference thoughtfully changed the rules to make a 55 per cent majority suffice for a strike, and decided to seek the biggest increases in the history of British coal mining – up to £9 a head. The Coal Board decided this was ridiculous. They offered a pound or two, the miners voted 59 per cent for striking, their president, Joe Gormley, said they were 'leading the battle against Government policy', and on 9 January 1972 the pits closed down. Fleet Street saw the miners as wrong-headed and doomed. So they might have been, if the stocks of coal that were theoretically available could have been moved where they were needed, and if oil-fired power stations had continued to receive supplies. But picketing was well organized. Railwaymen refused to move fuel trains. 'We were conscious, perhaps, of the failure of the railway unions to back the miners in 1926,' a Communist railwayman said to me solemnly. 'There was a desire not to allow ourselves to be used against the miners. We atoned for the failure of the previous generation.'

Behind the scenes moved the figure of Lawrence Daly, general secretary of the miners' union, and its most powerful official. Daly, a Scotsman, had held office for three years. He stood for the new militancy. He was to be seen touring London power stations with a bus-load of miners and their wives, meeting pickets and power supply workers, who were pursuing a claim of their own, with an overtime ban that made the electricity situation worse.* At one power station he told pickets that the miners were 'waging a struggle against the State-capitalist Coal Board', adding that their fight was 'one for the whole of the labour movement'.

Daly caught the mood of his miners and fed it back to them; the miners caught the mood of the union militants everywhere, who had been simmering at rising unemployment, painful inflation and the Industrial Relations Act. The Act, introduced in December 1970, and law since August 1971, had crystallized animosities towards the Government. Most unions had decided not to cooperate when it came into effect early in 1972. The TUC's annual meeting the previous September had been overshadowed by the Act. Hugh Scanlon for the engineers had said that cooperation would be fatal – 'a single scratch can lead to gangrene'. Daly had supported him. In January 1972 the unions were waiting to see how the Act would first be used against them. The miners' strike was about money. But it must have drawn some of its vigour from the movement's sense of grievance with the Tories and their policies. The picketing of power stations was more stringent than the Board had expected, so much so that the NUM became alarmed at bad publicity over a few incidents of violence, and Daly wrote urgently to area secretaries, reminding them that picketing must be peaceful.

In the event, a certain amount of rough picketing continued, but the authorities prudently chose not to make it an issue. The Coal Board later listed forty-two episodes of 'violent picketing',

*George Wake, who leads a militant power workers' group and is a member of the Communist Party national executive, says it was 'our ban on overtime and a work to rule that caused the blackouts'.

most of them involving white-collar staff trying to enter premises; men were kicked and spat on, bricks thrown, cars damaged.

Marches and rallies showed the miners maintaining their angry mood. A Gas Board coke depot at Saltley, in Birmingham, where lorries were coming from far afield to collect supplies, was closed by pickets after a week of incidents, ending with a march to Saltley by engineering workers holding a one-day sympathy strike. When helicopters were used to deliver hydrogen and other materials to power stations, one group of strikers seriously considered using homing pigeons to interfere with flights. The lunatic fringe, looking marginally less lunatic than it would have done twenty years before, was ready with helpful comments. The underground newspaper *Frendz* appeared with a feature headed 'Miners strike: dress rehearsal for the uprising?' This indicated how power cuts and mass unemployment would lead to revolution in the streets; a naive version* of the fantasies about bringing down the Government (together with any shaky bits of capitalism that would come down with it) that recurred throughout the year.

The reality was bad enough. By the time Wilberforce was appointed to head the court of inquiry, on 11 February, power stations were closing and substantial cuts were imminent. The Coal Board, but not the union, had agreed to be bound by the court's findings. The evidence was heard in two days in public, on 15 and 16 February. Lawrence Daly spoke for the miners; Derek Ezra, the chairman, for the Coal Board. The Board's submission, set out in fifty-four sheets of typescript, with appendices, listed the union's case as well as its own, and concluded that the men's claim was 'beyond all reason'. One of its tables showed that colliery workers earned four times as much as in 1947, against a $2\frac{1}{2}$ times increase in the cost of living. But the union's statistics for the relative worsening of their position, together with such ammunition as seven working miners who

*A sample paragraph: 'As the strike begins to bite even deeper, wildcat strikes, one-day stoppages, demonstrations in support will break out. At Social Security offices, people will queue for hours and there will be angry scenes, even riots as hundreds of angry workers try to claim benefits for the times they were off due to power cuts. Resentment grows against the Government for making such a balls of the whole deal ...'

were produced in the flesh by Daly, were too much for the Board. The Trade Union Research Unit at Ruskin marshalled the material, and John Hughes was present to ask awkward questions.

Instead of the traditional picture, miners confronted by hard-faced coal owners, it was rather the Coal Board confronted by hard-faced union. In one edgy exchange, Ezra suggested that the union's figures omitted benefits in kind, such as concessionary coal, to which Daly gave the corrosive reply: 'When I made references, as I have done in the last two or three weeks, to your salary of £20,000 a year, I was by no means taking into account, either for you or the other members of the Coal Board, the various perks that you receive on your job. The same with mining. These figures vary.' It didn't answer the question. Ezra's estimate that the concessions were worth £2.30 a head remained. But the Coal Board had no chance against the emotional charge of the miners' case.

Wilberforce and his colleagues finished hearing the evidence on a Wednesday, wrote their report on Thursday (setting what must be a speed record for courts of inquiry) and published it on Friday. It recommended increases of up to £6 a week, the agreement to run for sixteen months. The union refused to accept, judging shrewdly that the orange could be squeezed once more before it was dry. The talks moved to Downing Street, ending with a further bagful of concessions in the early hours of Saturday, that proved sufficient. The increases were worth something like 21 per cent over a year, three times the Coal Board's original offer.

They were won partly by intimidation, though the union wouldn't agree. The fact that the miners had a good case is not the whole story; other good cases go by the board. The postmen who said their pockets were picked felt they had a good case, too. The miners were able to extract an unprecedented sum from the Coal Board because they had the strength to back their arguments. They also provided the clearest realization, to date, of the often-heard fears that strikes at key points can be more damaging today than in the past. In 1921 the miners were out for nearly six months. But with industry and homes less dependent on centrally-generated electric power, the country managed well enough. In

1972, six weeks was enough to cause major disruption. The miners were using the weapon they had used so often before, but time had sharpened it.

Daly said it was 'the greatest victory in the miners' history'. It was also a personal victory for him. Later in the year miners' delegates at their annual conference heard the more moderate Gormley ask them not to have an annual confrontation over wages. Next day they heard Daly say that 'moderation in pursuit of justice is no virtue', and voted to demand a £7 increase and a reduction of hours for underground workers from thirty-seven to thirty. Another time bomb had begun to tick.

The new claims may have been among the items on the agenda for the N U M's national executive on the day, shortly before the 1972 conference, that I was supposed to meet Daly at union headquarters. The entrance hall is marbly and glassy. A black sculpture shows a near-naked man hewing coal. There were few signs of life, an impression that strengthened on later visits, as though the union's real business goes on elsewhere, at pit-heads and in working-men's clubs. I had telephoned Daly earlier in the morning to confirm the appointment. No one knew where he was until I reached the vice-president. He said that Mr Daly was in Yorkshire, but if he said he'd be here, he'd be here.

On the dot of 12.30 he appeared from the Euston Road and said he had driven with colleagues straight down the motorway after celebrating a union official's retirement; a short man with a shiny face and strong eyebrows, porkpie hat jammed on his head, carrying a bag. He left the bag and said that, if I didn't mind, some colleagues were in the pub round the corner, and why didn't we join them? On the way we passed a wall with the scrawled message: 'The tigers of wrath are wiser than the horses of instruction.' He stopped to read it aloud and said: 'That must have come from John Donne. It couldn't be anyone else, unless it's Dylan Thomas.' I had the wild thought that perhaps he had written it on the wall himself, and intended asking him in the pub. But after accepting a lager and a whisky from someone else, and introducing me to a group who were buying pints and hot lunches, he vanished, leaving his drinks untouched on the table, and never came back.

Among the group was Michael McGahey, president of the Scottish miners and member of the National Executive, a lean man with a sober voice and didactic manner who stretched across and gripped my knees with fingers like iron when I said I was writing about industrial relations. 'It's not industrial relations, by the way,' he said. 'It happens to be class relations. It's us and them.'

They were like men acting like militants, amused at their own harshness, proud of such long memories. They had all been to the overnight shindig and were on their way to the executive meeting. A Yorkshireman described the scene: 'Four hundred pensioners, some of them decrepit, some of them bearing their age well – men who've given their lives to the industry, and now they're shoved to one side with a fucking thirty shillings a week pension. You know what the miner was like in the 1920s? He lived like an animal. Now his standard of living has advanced, so do you know what? They'll bribe him. We've got men on the executive who can be bought out with a meal and a bottle of wine. It's a fact.'

McGahey, who is a Communist, on the party's National Executive, told me a joke about a manager who says he'll give a young lad a job if he can detect which is the manager's glass eye. The boy points to it at once. 'How did you know?' says the manager. 'There's more sympathy in that one,' says the boy. McGahey laughed and put down his knife and fork. 'Industrial relations,' he said, 'is going to sharpen in terms of class conflict. I remember talking to Barbara Castle at a Scottish T U C meeting after her White Paper, "In Place of Strife", and I said, "Barbara, there is only one paragraph that I agree with, and that is the first one that says there are necessarily conflicts of interest in industry."'

A month later I saw Daly in his office. He said he was sorry about the last time, but he had been called away. Without his hat he looked more pugnacious. I had the obvious questions to ask. In 1969 Daly wrote in the *Political Quarterly* about two possible views of trade unions – one, that they should cooperate with the State in decision-making, the other, that they should assert themselves as a 'potential instrument of social revolution'. His sympathies were obviously with the second. He wrote:

For many the lesson is that the movement should formulate ideas about the society it would like ultimately to see, and be less satisfied with minimal short-term objectives: more demands and less compromise.

He concluded:

When men (or women) decide to withdraw their labour it is usually because experience has taught them that silent pain evokes no response. It may well be that protest and disturbance will remain always with us. But to the extent that it expresses the striving of working people for economic and social justice it is to be welcomed. More so, if, at the same time, it impels us in the direction of a more genuinely democratic society than we know today.

Daly was an early member of the editorial board of the *New Left Review*, and was active in the New Left movement in the 1950s. He left the Communist Party in 1956. What concerned him (he said to me) was the concentration of economic power and wealth in fewer hands, as the modern State grew more centralized and bureaucratic. 'While I'm certainly not an anarchist, or anything like it,' he said, 'I'm certainly not in favour of compromising with anyone in Government or industry for the continuing unequal distribution of wealth. That would not be socialism.'

If that was the theory, where was the action? He said the unions' traditional radicalism was becoming influential again, and referred me to the wider effects of today's radicalism – on the young, or in countries like Czechoslovakia. A deeper compassion was apparent, a concern for the underdog. Was there an element of wishful thinking and romanticism in this? He said that certainly he was conditioned by his memories, by his upbringing in a village where the miners and their families were treated as chattels, where 'the only way to strength was to try to get a hundred per cent membership of the union, and be prepared to withdraw our labour. It sounds old-fashioned, but I still hold the views I held in my teens.' It was one reason he was so opposed to the Industrial Relations Act; it threatened the closed shop and thus the bargaining strength of the unions.

Finally, what about industrial action for political ends? Daly first dismissed the idea that there had been anything political about the recent strike: it was a strike for justice. Then he said that a strike aimed at removing the Industrial Relations Act from the statute book would not be political. The Act was designed to weaken the unions, and 'my personal view is that we would be morally justified in taking industrial action to have that law removed'. In the same way, strikes intended to bring down the Government at the time of Suez in 1956 would have been completely justified, and so would strikes in the near future in opposition to the Government's housing finance legislation.

It seemed a comprehensive list. Daly is patient, rational, thinks carefully before he speaks, and leads a close-knit union that appears, on recent evidence, to provide a machine for translating ideas into action. In one sense he told me nothing; in another, everything. He is a natural man for a battlefield.

4. The Strategists

It would be unreasonable to see in the unions more than streaks and patches of hell-bent militancy. They are not marching forward shoulder to shoulder, singing that 'the people's flag is deepest red'. Dockers don't all want violence. Draughtsmen and supervisors are not all like the men of DATA (now TASS) at Vauxhall Motors, who objected to redundancy notices by having a Day of Thought (when they all sat and thought about their work), followed by a Day of Cleanliness (tidying desks and drawers) and a Day of Meditation (queuing for the lavatories). Only a minority of workers have ever occupied the factory or the shipyard.

The trade-union movement seen from the inside is heavy with orthodox men who plod along orthodox paths. They call one another – in speeches, formal statements and the union journals – 'Brother' and 'Sister', perhaps reflecting the chapel influences in early trade unionism; the Communists' 'Comrade' has never caught on. Many union leaders are offered and accept titles. The General Council of the TUC has a life peer and a knight,* as well as a liberal sprinkling of C.B.E.s and O.B.E.s. To workers on the far left, this calls for censure. The *Socialist Worker*, published by the International Socialists – a Marxist group that is stronger among students and intellectuals than on the factory floor – never tires of attacking the 'trade-union bureaucrats'. Vic Feather (C.B.E.), the mild secretary of the TUC, is shown puffing a cigar, with the caption: 'In the big time'. Even Jack Jones (M.B.E.) of the TGWU, a troubling figure on suburban television screens, is well to the right when viewed by those who are far to the left.

*Lord Cooper, General and Municipal Workers (who retires at the end of 1972). Sir Sidney Greene, National Union of Railwaymen.

Some of the largest unions are still regarded as 'right-wing', though they usually resent the description as suggesting they are ineffectual. The G M W U (third biggest, 850,000 members), with a strong father-and-son tradition among officials, would like to shed its old paternalism. David Basnett, the national officer, says: 'I would accept that we are caricatured as a right-wing union, and I would accept there is some justification. We say we should strike less frequently. But we say we should seek positive changes by the hard graft of negotiation rather than the easier route of militant action.'

The other big union identified with the right is the electricians', in full the Electrical Electronic Telecommunication and Plumbing Union, or E E T P U. This is the fifth biggest, with 420,000 members. It is a union with a past. As the Electrical Trades Union it was the subject of a lawsuit in 1961 which found that the Communists who controlled it had rigged an election to have their nominee appointed general secretary. He was deposed by the court and, since 1964, Communists have been banned from holding office. The general secretary now is Frank Chapple, a plaintiff in the 1961 lawsuit against the Communists, and earlier still a Communist himself for seventeen years; he is a natural target for the far left. 'The clearest period of my life was when I was in the party,' he says. 'Ideologically it suits a lot of people – not the "ism" itself but the idea that things are cut and dried. I haven't known since I left where I stand in the ideological spectrum, and I don't think it matters all that much. I swing about, making practical decisions. I would say the line I take in negotiations, and the policy I am in agreement with, more closely represent what the bulk of ordinary people think and want.'

Chapple is a dark, energetic man who would pass for a self-employed electrician or plumber whose time is costing him money. He calls for a hot fish sandwich in his office, and it arrives steaming on the plate, accompanied by a pot of mahogany tea. 'What I've said to the revolutionaries in our union is,' he says, 'do you want the bloody union to fall apart? Or do you want a union that's getting somewhere? I said only this morning, those of you who believe in confrontation may get a government of

Enoch Powells, not one of Scanlons and Joneses. I don't mean I wouldn't have any confrontations. Strikes are better than revolutions, and sometimes, in modern conditions, a strike is the first time a man's been able to influence this bloody awful machine. But confrontation over what I consider to be justifiable claims by members, which is usually based on the contributions they've made. I don't take up an ideological position on incentives or manning or creating efficiency. I'll take up a position when I find the electricity supply workers are likely to end up getting a marginal return for the contribution we've made. There's bound to be a confrontation on that, incidentally. People like me are regarded as expendable by the establishment – they say, "He's a good guy, he'll always agree in the end." Well, that's not always true.'

Chapple's philosophy sees a union as a day-to-day business, making the best of situations, accepting that some wage claims will do better than others. He doesn't go on about building a new society ('I'm not clear what the end product should be, except not fascist and not Communist'), preferring to point to things as they are. He observes unions that are 'not powerful enough to protect their members – look at the sections of workers who get exploited, like women and young people, or the disparities in wages between one industry and another'. Chapple's views are no longer fashionable. It is the militants who hypnotize reporters. 'Press and TV put me through the meat grinder,' says Chapple. 'The Joneses and Scanlons are portrayed as nice men. The most ridiculous side of this coin is the adulation of Jimmy Reid over Upper Clyde Shipbuilders. The fact that he had been a full-time organizer for the Communist Party was obscured on TV. He turns up whiter than white, like a knight on a charger.' Chapple drops constant hints about the influences he suspects below the surface. Television's weakness for militant trade unionists may be because 'there are forces at work'. There may be 'some deep political purpose' behind certain wage claims. He adds: 'I'm a bit obsessed with this, but ...' – then laughs, and the sentence fades away.

Chapple is probably right when he says that a pragmatic approach to wage claims suits most union members. It is the underlying mood that he seems to ignore, a sense of discontent, ready to be played upon. Extreme militants are in a minority (they always are) but for the moment the tide is running in their direction. It is a careful, even a discreet militancy. But union leaders like Jones, Scanlon and Clive Jenkins are the ones who will be remembered, in their different ways, as typical of the times.

An important part of the new strategy is the movement for 'shop-floor democracy'. The phrase means different things to different people, from mild forms of participation by employers to full-blooded workers' control. There is even an Institute for Workers' Control, founded in 1968 with money from the Bertrand Russell Peace Foundation. It operates from Nottingham (and now pays its own way) as a focus of radical thinking and advice, with a mixed bag of members whose fingers are in various political pies. It has numerous Marxist adherents. 'Workers' control', says one of its publications, 'begins with simple trade-union demands, for control of hiring and firing, tea-breaks, hours, speeds of work, allocation of jobs, and so on. It mounts through a whole series of demands (open the books, for example) to a point where, ultimately, over the whole of society, capitalist authority meets impasse.'

The movement has to do with the conditions of work, mental and physical. 'Once you ding that clock,' says a shop steward, 'all your rights have gone. Nobody asks you about the design of the shop. Nobody asks you what colour it'll be painted.' The idea that anyone should ask, let alone take notice of the answer, may seem eccentric. But once the subject is raised, it has to be argued. Sickness-absenteeism increases year by year; either the nation's health is collapsing, or people use illness as an excuse to take more time off work.* There must be massive malingering. But it is a means of retrieving some control. It may be costing you money, but it's your own life you're running.

Money is the first and most important thing the workers want

*Between 1954 and 1970, days lost through sickness rose from 280 million to 342 million; the increase represents a year's work by a quarter of a million men. Summer months show the sharpest increase. The 1971 figure will be lower, perhaps because National Insurance benefit for the first three days of sickness is no longer payable.

to control. By negotiating their own rates, on top of whatever national agreements exist, factory workers can feel they are slightly more in command of their affairs. The 'wages drift' of the last twenty years, so unwelcome to Governments and so natural to workers, has had its roots in plant-by-plant bargaining backed by the threat of unofficial strikes. 'For thirty years,' says Scanlon, 'we had relatively full employment. In that situation we realized that when taking aggressive action, the power resides on the shop floor. It's always been the union's job to build a skeleton composed of basic rates, and to say to the lads on the shop floor, put some flesh on it.'

The car industry is the classic example. This is where militant wage strategies have been pushed ahead, mainly by members of the TGWU and the AUEW. Their strikes have been monotonously seen as unpatriotic. But to car workers it is a matter of pride that they are well ahead of others in engineering. At Longbridge, Birmingham, British Leyland's biggest plant, average earnings of manual workers are £38 a week; something like three-quarters of a million pounds is brought in under guard to make up the pay packets. The wages are not as sensational as the years of conflict might suggest. Managements were willing to pay the rates because there was so much competition for labour at a time of full employment. An article in The *Financial Times*, noting the strong position of British car manufacturers in Europe, remarks in passing that 'wage costs are relatively low'.* But they are higher than they would have been without the conflict. A production man on the 'track', where cars progress from skeleton to finished model, can earn £50 or £60 by working overtime or at night. Maintenance fitters can earn the same. Ten miles away will be fitters with similar skills earning barely half as much.

Shop-floor haggling has been most marked at British Leyland, where, unlike Ford and Vauxhall, the production workers have been paid on a piecework basis. Every time a new model or refinement of an old model was introduced, the shop stewards would bargain for a better rate. Originally the piecework system suited the manufacturers. But that was between the wars, when the workers at car plants were traditionally casual labour, well

*'Hard days for Europe's carmakers', James Ensor, 19 July 1972.

paid but 'in and out of jobs like yo-yos, a completely dehuman-
ized system' – as a senior labour relations man at British Leyland
now describes it. Later on, as the car workers became better
organized and stronger, they turned the system round and exploited it. Dick Etheridge, convenor and leading shop steward
at Longbridge, remarks that 'in the war we said, bugger it, if
the job isn't worth it, we ain't going to do it. That's the attitude
today. After the war we were able to push the prices up, and we
got what they call wages drift, what we call bargaining power.
We reckon it's worth a pound a year per man.'

Management saw it as a ritualistic haggling that looked for any
excuse to adjust the rates upwards. The record for chronic trouble
at a British Leyland plant, and probably in the British car industry, is held by the assembly plant at Cowley, Oxford. In 1969
there were 612 separate stoppages, an average of 2.6 for each
working day, and an estimated 33,000 vehicles were lost. The
following year was much the same. A constant battle over
prices became part of the system; sometimes it was carried to
extremes, but it was not an accident; it was meant to be like that.
One of the long-standing advocates of local piecework bargaining
is Jack Jones, who spent sixteen years in the Midlands as a
TGWU district official, helping to introduce it. 'When I
arrived,' he once said,* 'there were all sorts of malpractice in the
motor industry. The unions had no control over pieceworking,
although that was the main system of payment. There was a
great deal of discrimination and personal favouritism, particularly
by the foremen, and special merit payments to the blue-eyed
boys. We built up trade union organization to change all that.'

In the last year or two British Leyland has been trying to persuade its workers to give up piecework in place of fixed wages.
'Basically,' says Pat Lowry, the director of industrial relations,
'it's a question of management trying to bring back to itself some
control of operations.' The unions call it 'measured day-work',
a phrase carefully avoided by British Leyland, in case it sounds
like spies with stop-watches. A cartoon in *Carworker*, a Marxist
newspaper in the industry, shows a worker looking with interest
at a carrot labelled 'MDW' that suddenly becomes a pair of

*Interview in the *Guardian*, 9 November 1968.

jaws that seize him by the testicles. 'MDW – the carrot that BITES BACK!' reads the caption.

Where fixed rates have been introduced, it has been after months of argument about 'mutuality', the mutual agreement between unions and management over the amount of work that should be established as the norm for an hour or a day. The unions have been reluctant to have piecework prised away from them, although the amount of wages lost by their own disputes has turned some against it – over one long period, the working week in parts of the Cowley plant averaged only thirty-two hours. 'One of the virtues of the piecework system is that it's a substitute for management,' says a TGWU official at Cowley. 'They set the rates and agree them with the shop stewards, and the lads run it themselves. So there's an element of individual rights and control over the system. If you want you can work like stink one day and take it easy the next. If you allow management to introduce measured day-work, you may be returning to the brown boots and bowler hat brigade on the shop floor. Therefore we sought an agreement which, while it got rid of piecework, didn't give management the control it was seeking. We injected mutuality.'

One of the Cowley agreements, dated February 1971, devotes three-quarters of its text to mutuality. The paragraph headed 'Performance' begins: 'Standard performance, i.e. effort, shall be mutually agreed on the basis of normal output without over-exertion, with due consideration to fatigue and the need for an agreed amount of personal time.' By introducing ideas like 'normal output' and 'over-exertion', the unions open up whole areas for continuing debate. Dick Etheridge at Longbridge (where fixed rates are still being rejected by the workers) says that 'management's in trouble over measured day-work because they can't make the lads work at the pace they want them to. The pace is well below.' He adds the unwelcome thought for British Leyland that 'any system will be controlled by shop stewards, and the shop floor, once they get the hang of it'.

The line between 'unions' and 'shop stewards' is blurred, in the car industry or anywhere else. The shop stewards belong to unions but may act independently of the local branch. This is the hazy area that caused trouble over dockers in 1972 – were their shop stewards officials of the union, who could be disciplined by headquarters if they broke the law under the Industrial Relations Act, or were they (as Jack Jones and the TGWU insisted) independent spokesmen for their fellows? It is in the interests of employers, Governments and all who believe in the status quo to have clearly identified union officials, responsible for their members, who can be argued with and if necessary prosecuted for illegal acts. It is in the interests of the workers to make themselves amorphous – a shifting body of men who can apply pressure where and when it suits them, and who can act with the authority of officials without being legally liable for their acts. This is the so-called 'anarchy' that the militants are accused of encouraging (Frank Chapple, in the moderate camp, talks of 'discipline' among his members, and says firmly that his union is responsible for its shop stewards). The Industrial Relations Act is an attempt, mismanaged so far, to compel unions to behave like hierarchies, with a top-to-bottom structure that fits nicely into the industrial system. It collides head-on with the ideas of shop-floor democracy.

Hugh Scanlon of the engineers appears even more committed to the shop-floor philosophy than Jack Jones. Jones has the reputation of being a careful operator who believes in the art of the possible; a colder fish who handles each side of his big union, from trawlermen and dockers to busmen and garage repairers, in the way that seems most expedient. Scanlon excites warmer comments. 'Hughie is the little trustworthy revolutionary,' says a civil servant who has had dealings with him. Like Jones, he was a militant when it was less fashionable than it is now. His background is industrial Manchester, though he was born in Australia, where his parents had emigrated, in 1913. His father, an upholsterer, died soon afterwards, and his widow brought her children back to Lancashire. Hugh Scanlon began work at fourteen, as an apprentice at Metropolitan Vickers. He was a shop steward at twenty-two, a Communist at twenty-three, a rising figure in the local Amalgamated Engineering Union before he was thirty. He was steeped in the ways of a union with deep traditions and long memories, living in the city where the oldest industrial working class in the world began. As the Amalgamated Society of Engineers, founded in 1851 from a number of smaller bodies, it was among the first of the modern unions. The engineers, then and now the base of British industrial wealth, were appointing shop stewards and bargaining over piecework before the end of the nineteenth century. Scanlon's Manchester doesn't forget its past. At Peterloo, now lost in the city centre, the workers were cut about by the cavalry one hot summer's afternoon. Engels saw his smoky vision of the working class in Manchester. The Trades Union Congress was founded there; the Cooperative movement began ten miles away at Rochdale.

The message of his background for Scanlon has been that the shop-floor is where the action is, or should be. He has called it 'one of the most deplorable aspects of trade unionism over the past decade or so, that the shop steward has been maligned almost as much by the trade union leadership as by the press and employers'.* He has spoken often about the need for industrial democracy, by which he means the full-blooded version, with factory committees to appoint the managers, and 'full and detailed information concerning costing, marketing and all other essential financial details'† to help shop stewards negotiate on equal terms. In 1972 he helped to generate an extraordinary series of local strikes that lasted for months – a muddled episode that reflects the muddled intricacies of shop-floor democracy.

It began with a sweeping demand for more money as a reward for doing less work. Scanlon presented it in the summer of 1971 with cheerful pertinacity. He is a traditional trade-union figure, like something from the past with a few modifications to bring him up to date; he dislikes the bosses heartily, distrusts the mass media (but uses them when it suits him), and speaks bluntly about what concerns him. 'In finality,' he will say, 'we will win battles because we can last without food longer than the employers can do without labour. It's a crude way of putting it, but it's true.' In 1971 his union and its associates in the Confederation of Shipbuilding and Engineering Unions put in a claim for

---

New Left Review, 1967.

†'Workers' Control and the Transnational Company', Pamphlet No. 22, Institute for Workers' Control.

'substantial' increases all round, a rise in the minimum rate of £5 or £6, an extra week's holiday and a working week of thirty-five hours instead of forty. The package was tentatively costed as being worth a 40 per cent increase, excluding a demand for equal pay for women that was hopefully written off as a gesture. The Engineering Employers' Federation made despairing noises. It said the claim was not realistic and would bankrupt many firms.

In themselves the increases in minimum rates were not crucial, since few engineering workers earn the minimum: plant bargaining has pushed the level up. This discrepancy between minimum rates and actual rates confuses innocent newspaper readers, who see, as in the 1971–2 episode, that the engineering unions want to raise the rate for an unskilled worker from £15 to £20. Some workers were paid as little as £15, but not many. When Scanlon appearing on television says to an employer, 'And you're proud of the fact that your industry offers a labourer £15 a week?',* he is putting it at its worst for the sake of the argument. But the minimum rate is the one used to compute holiday, shift and overtime pay; and it is the base from which local bargaining begins. The employers responded with an all-round offer of £1.50, described by Scanlon, as 'provocative', and by the end of the year the talks had collapsed. The negotiating machinery set up fifty years earlier between employers and unions was swept aside, and the engineers, through their national committee of members from each division, decided to press their claims locally; factory-by-factory bargaining on a national scale.

The result was widespread confusion. More than three million engineering workers were involved, directly and indirectly. The A U E W, a union with elaborate 'democratic' procedures, found itself at the centre of what might or might not eventually amount to nation-wide stoppages, which it had sanctioned and now could do little about. At union headquarters in Peckham, south London, which has roses up the path and stained glass in the door, right- and left-wing factions were disagreeing among themselves. Scanlon's mail was heavy. The woman who sends him giant postcards pasted over with headlines and photographs from newspapers had written to Joe Gormley of the miners'

*'Summertalk', BBC TV, 21 July 1972.

union, c/o Hugh Scanlon. 'We are all proud as peacocks,' she wrote. 'I have waited a lifetime for men such as you and Mr Scanlon to throw down the gauntlet of unmistakable words to the greedy capitalists.' There is a homely headquarters atmosphere in Peckham that is common among trade unions, the feeling of a low-powered family business with everyone on first-name terms. Until a year ago every general secretary of the engineers was obliged to live in a house adjoining the offices; the rules had to be changed to let him move away. A recent incumbent could be glimpsed by the typists stealing out in pyjamas to collect the papers and the milk. Mixed with the homely atmosphere was a sense of threat. The accountants were counting the funds – £14 million in all, with more than £11 million irrevocably set aside to make it untouchable by the courts in the event of trouble with the Industrial Relations Act, and consequently untouchable by the union for use in industrial actions, ever. The year before, the A U E W had spent £1½ million on pay for local strikers; financing a national strike is out of the question for a union with nearly a million and a half members.

It was left to the union's 2,800 branches and 36,000 shop stewards to decide what exactly to do about squeezing the employers. Most of them decided to do nothing, to the disgust of the militants, but enough of them acted to produce results. The industrial democrats, half-hearted in most areas, began to take action in March in the north-west of England, centred on Manchester. Here, in Scanlon country, the centre of heavy engineering, overtime bans and work-to-rules were imposed at dozens of factories. The A U E W's Manchester divisional organizer, the job that used to be Scanlon's, is John Tocher. He is a Communist, and so is the Manchester district secretary, Bernard Panter, together with another full-time district official, making three officials out of six who are members of the C P. As Tocher points out, they don't conceal their politics, and the votes for action were taken at mass meetings of shop stewards. 'Somebody called us the Manchester bloody mafia,' he says. 'We object to that. It's libellous. The employers are the real mafia.'

A few employers settled quickly. Several were held to have let the side down, and were expelled from the employers' association. Tocher showed me a couple of agreements, keeping his hand over the names of the companies, with all-round increases of £3 and £4. One company conceded a 38½-hour week, to the horror of other employers, who got to hear about it, and saw it as the thin end of the wedge. The agreement containing the one-and-a-half-hours concession read: 'To achieve this, the normal starting time will be 8.18 a.m. instead of 8 a.m.'; like many union victories, it seems a trifling benefit when it's spread so thin.

Most of the Manchester victories were even thinner. Employers took a strong line. They set up a fund to help small firms, and adopted a policy of suspending workers and closing the plant when production was interfered with. The workers retaliated by occupying factories, using the technique of 'sit-ins' and 'work-ins'. These had rarely occurred in Britain before the workers at Upper Clyde Shipbuilders took over their yard (for a period) in 1971, but had been used half a dozen times since then. The value seems to be psychological more than anything, offering at first sight the shadow of industrial democracy without the substance, but contributing to morale and the feeling of 'solidarity' that milit-ants crave for, and at the same time lowering the spirits of the employers. Soon thirty or forty plants had been, or were being, occupied. It was impossible ever to get a clear picture of what was happening. A modest slice of the engineering industry was thrown out of action, but the scene changed constantly as settle-ments were made or more factories came out. The Manchester employers estimated that at the height of the sit-ins, not more than 20,000 of 150,000 workers were affected.

It was the UK record to date for workers' participation via direct action. Like so many British occasions, it was difficult to see how much violent reality, if any, was concealed behind the rules by which everyone agreed the game should be played. One small firm applied for a writ to get its factory back from the twenty-two workers who were occupying it. The judge complied, adding that if it were a bigger factory he would have thought twice in case police with tear gas were needed. Bailiffs and police visited the plant, without much success; later the company closed down.

Seen at close quarters, a sit-in was a stirring event for the sitters, enabling them to clutch at reality and prove they mattered to the great industrial machine. Or that was the illusion. I went to Timperley, in Cheshire, on the edge of the Manchester industrial belt. On the iron gates to the plant, facing a towpath and canal, were two notices. One offered good pay and security for workers with the Metal Box Co. The other said 'Official sit-in' in red paint, with '11th week' chalked underneath, and under that again, 'Shit or bust'. The two company security men stayed inside their cubicle. They were not in charge of the gates. The workers, who presently drifted back from a meeting inside the factory, decided who came in and went out.

Earlier in the sit-in there had been a ridiculous confrontation between workers and managers, both sides using chains, padlocks and bolt-cutters to fasten the gates shut (the workers) or open (the managers). Police watched sympathetically while men snipped away and lengths of broken chain accumulated. That phase was over. So was the regrettable incident when management cut off the electricity and locked the lavatories. The management people got locked in as a punishment; one of them was there for, it was thought, eighty-nine hours. 'They were virtually prisoners in their own factory,' said a sitter, relishing the words and repeating them: 'Prisoners *in their own factory*'.

The senior shop steward was John Roylance, aged thirty, strongly built, with heavy cheeks and remarkable furry sideburns, like an experiment for a new sort of beard. In purple trousers and a bright blue shirt that matched his slightly bulging eyes, with curly hair combed forward to project in a roll like dark sheep's wool above his forehead, he was a man with a physical presence, which is an asset for a shop steward. He admitted losing his temper with the management at one fiery meeting, and threatening to wreck the place. Bernard Panter, the district secretary, was there, and calmed him down. 'I didn't mean to actually do anything,' said Roylance, 'but it gets too much for you.' The sit-in excited him, the more he talked about it. 'It's fantastic, what we've done, what we've gone through,' he said. 'There's one of the lads, normally he can't get to work by a quarter to eight. He's no use at getting up in the morning. Now he gets here at six. It's in the blood now, you can't get it out.

When it's over, I don't know what I'm going to do. It gets you. It's definitely in my blood.'

The work-force was 140 strong, divided into shifts to occupy the plant twenty-four hours a day. They had light, heat, radio, television and the canteen; they played cards, darts, chess, football and cricket. The object, they said, was not merely psychological. Management might get up to its tricks and try moving things out in the backs of cars. The plant produced machine tools for the canning industry. Some were half built – they pointed them out, giant suites of metal furniture lined up in the shadows. With the factory occupied, they said, management didn't dare touch a screw.

After eleven weeks, both sides should have had enough. No one else had been sitting in for eleven weeks. The meeting that morning had been to put management's latest offer to the shop-floor, with the stewards advising against it, but not optimistic of their chances. But seventy-four had voted against accepting, with forty-one in favour. 'I was amazed,' said Roylance. 'With today's offer the women would have been on fifteen to twenty pounds, which is bloody good money.' He would have been earning £33 for a forty-hour week (his basic rate remained £25). 'But what did I get?' he said. 'A vote of confidence from the lads. I felt bloody bad when I went in there, but why should we worry now? We'll break records.'

'Don't say that,' said an older man. 'My wife will break my bloody head.'

The older man was not for going back, though. He said he had been learning things this year. He had learned there were similar factories within twenty miles where the rates were better than at Timperley. He had thought, for the first time in his life, about how much money he was entitled to. 'I've been in engineering for thirty-five years,' he said, 'and when the union put in for five pounds across the board, I thought, perhaps I'm worth more than I'm getting. I don't want to be given a rise just because the cost of living has gone up. When Edward Heath says to keep it down to 7 per cent he doesn't realize there are people thinking they should get more *anyway*, never mind the cost of living.'

He didn't sound militant; just puzzled and a trifle angry, with dawning suspicions. Roylance, on the other hand, sounded as if he had been born suspicious of managements and their ways. He loved anecdotes that showed them coming off second best. When the Duke of Windsor died not long before, the men had asked for a Union Jack to fly at half-mast. The management said they didn't have one. 'Too mean,' explained Roylance. So they got a sheet, painted the flag on it, and flew it from the company mast. Nor could he resist telling me about the false alarm call concerning a bomb on the premises that brought police, fire brigade and press. He told me who had made the call. Sit-ins needed publicity, he said, and this had been one way of getting it.

The union wasn't mentioned much at Timperley: it was their sit-in, not Hugh Scanlon's. One of the unresolved problems for a union which believes in shop-floor democracy is that the more the workers do for themselves, the greater the gulf between them and headquarters. Roylance was quoted in *Socialist Worker* as saying they had been let down by the union. Perhaps an active trade union must expect to live in a state of tension between the centre and the periphery. John Tocher in the divisional office had sharp differences of opinion with headquarters, just as workers at factories had sharp differences with the divisional office.

One of the less-militant plants that were in the majority, even in Manchester, was Mather & Platt, a large engineering firm whose shop stewards asked for a lot, as instructed, and settled for a little. This brought down the wrath of the divisional office, without effect. When I was there, the draughtsmen members of TASS were on strike over a claim of their own, and picketing the gates, but the rest of the plant was working. Jaguars and Rovers were lined up outside the offices. At reception three men wearing lightweight suits were chatting in that managerial way, quietly one minute and then booming out loud with a joke. In his ground-floor office with sporting prints on the wall, Edward Morton, personnel director and president of the local engineering employers' association, described the more or less successful outcome of the affair as seen from Mather & Platt.

This is where militant strategies run into the ground. We sat at his negotiating table, where the shop stewards had presented their claim in March, on the day that shop stewards all over Manchester were presenting theirs. 'They rushed in everywhere,' says Morton, 'some of them boldly, some of them laughingly, some of them sheepishly, and handed in their claim. Here, they were rather sheepish. I said, "You don't expect us to give you all that, do you?" and they said, "The district committee said we had to ask you."'

Morton, an ebullient middle-aged Welshman in a well-cut brown suit with matching handkerchief, described how the national talks between employers and unions had broken down the previous year. He gave a brief, cynical introduction to management strategies; another kind of reality. 'The unions said, 'You name a sum, and we will tell you by how much it falls short." It emerged they were asking for £25 basic for skilled men – remember, £25 basic can often represent a £45 wage. We said we weren't going to pay anything like that, and after a short time Mr Scanlon, who had been grappling with us for several years over negotiating procedures anyway, packed his bags and walked off.

'He was encouraged to do this by the history of what are laughingly called productivity bargains, notably in the motor industry. These were speeded up during the wages freeze as a means of giving men a rise. Companies wanted to get round the freeze because their competitors were doing it, and at that time they were all competing hard for skilled labour, and had been for years. The motor industry has an immense amount of capital equipment – the price of labour is frankly only a small part of total costs. So thousands of bogus productivity agreements were drawn up, with fellows promising the earth. They got some very good bargains, too.

'A lot of it's ghastly bloody work. Every time a car goes past, you dive into the boot and put the petrol pump in. Or you're a moulder in a foundry, making two cylinder blocks a minute. Either you use people of very low mentality, or people who've got time to think and brood and demand more money. Or Sikhs – those foundries in the Midlands are full of Sikhs. Anyway, from this the inflationary settlements stemmed.'

Morton said that when the claim arrived in March, he refused to discuss matters like holidays and hours, arguing that these were always decided nationally. He settled down to twenty hours of 'straight horse-trading', spread over three weeks. The offer finally agreed was equivalent to £2.30 a week, the agreement to run until August 1973. It was accepted at a mass meeting, but was rejected by the union's Manchester office. Bernard Panter wrote to the shop stewards refusing to approve the agreement and telling them to ask for more. 'They came and said, "We've been instructed by the district committee to unsign that agreement,"' said Morton, 'and I said, "Sorry, mate, once it's signed, it's signed."'

He talked about Scanlon, whom he had often met in national negotiations, and said that on the golf course he could be taken for a company director. He talked about negotiating and its effect on character. 'You never say "Yes",' he said. 'You never actually say, "Bugger off". You need an official interpreter. I met Ben Warris the comedian the other day. I shared a flat with him once, thirty years ago. He said, "You've changed." I said, "Yes, I've got older." "It's not that," he said. "You never answer a question directly."'

The wider question of what the engineers achieved is hard to answer. As a national strategy it was disastrous. The union was wrong about the militancy of its members, which was less than expected, and the militancy of the employers, which was greater. At Timperley the men held out for fifteen weeks, well into July, before accepting an offer of £3 all round, including women; a reasonable figure, though not what they hoped for. The general level of plant settlements was lower. But the persistence of the minority may have influenced the wider settlement that was eventually reached in August, when the wheel came full circle, back to national bargaining. The unions got the bigger basic rates they had wanted all along, with more for women to bring them nearer equal pay, and a couple of extra days' holiday. It was a long way from the success that Scanlon had hoped for. Local negotiations, no doubt, would continue as before.

An unknown number of workers will have looked more critically at their life and hard times, like the men at Timperley. Industrial democracy may have advanced a little by having its principles advertised and put into effect in a well-publicized way. It is difficult to put a finger on anything. The Institute for Workers' Control, running seminars and conferences attended by activists from the left, is as near as one is likely to get to seeing the fluttering ideas of shop-floor democracy pinned down. 'We are subversives,' says Ken Coates, the ex-miner (and Labour Party member) who is its chief spokesman, 'but not in the way some people think.' Even in the staid hierarchy of Lord Cooper's union, the GMWU, they talk about industrial democracy. David Basnett talks of the need for a breakthrough to bring more of the worker's life within his control – 'Why the hell shouldn't he discuss investment planning and manpower planning?'

Everywhere, as usual, there is more talk than action. Militants are a minority. For every Timperley there are a dozen Mather & Platts. But under the surface, moods and strategies are changing.

5. White-Collar Men

Clive Jenkins, best known of the white-collar leaders, has a concealed panic button on his desk that will sound an alarm and bring police aid to union headquarters in Camden Town. It is typical of Jenkins to have it installed. But it points to the changes at this end of the movement, that such a device might be remotely necessary.

White-collar workers increase daily. It is where more and more of the action will be found. These are truisms, and have been for years, but the old habit of regarding clerks and supervisors as a different and marginal kind of trade unionist persists, while the evidence for it shrinks. One third of British union members are now office, as opposed to factory, workers. The balance will continue to swing away from manual workers as teachers, salesmen and computer-programmers inherit the earth.

Uneasiness among middle-class professional workers at the thought of being in the same game as all those rough persons who keep going on strike will diminish. It turns out to be everybody's game. Manual workers, especially the lowest-paid, have improved their situation faster than many office workers have been able to do. In areas where secretaries and typists are in demand, such as London and the south-east, salaries of £1,200 or even £1,500, paid to bright girls barely into their twenties, have narrowed another gap. As inflation and large pay increases distort old differentials, the professional worker who goes on his quiet way without an organization to help him is sure to lose. This is the essential appeal of white-collar unionism.

The National Union of Teachers (230,000 working members) didn't affiliate to the T U C until 1970 because of a lingering feeling that it meant joining the cloth caps. It somehow contradicted the teachers' life-work of helping bright boys to rise out of their poor backgrounds and become something better, like teachers. The feeling still lingers among older members, but counts for little now. The results of collective bargaining by an active union are too visible. The effect is felt well up the salary-scale, so that although the earnings of many white-collar workers are not so far above factory-work levels, executives earning £5,000 and £6,000 a year have their salaries negotiated for them.

The National Union of Bank Employees (100,000 members) has something under one-fifth of the managers at Lloyds and the Midland, two-fifths at Barclays. The local bank manager, all-powerful behind his frosted glass, could be earning £3,500, 30 per cent of it negotiated for him by his union over the past two or three years. Airline pilots, with salaries up to £9,500, are un-inhibited about pressing their claims via the British Airline Pilots Association. Clive Jenkins says that ASTMS, the Association of Scientific, Technical and Managerial Staffs (280,000 members), negotiates for a few individuals earning as much as £7,000 – 'worth £10,000 with perks', adds Jenkins, who has a fine eye for financial detail.

Jenkins, as everyone knows, is something new in trade union-ism, pursuing salary claims with sophisticated comparisons and arguments, and much ferocity. The white-collar field is wide. At one end are the broadly non-technical men and women – teachers, doctors, administrators, managers, clerks and office workers in general. At the other end are the technical categories – draughtsmen, chemists, laboratory staffs, computer technolo-gists, shop-floor supervisors and formen. Jenkins's union is scooping them all in, those who would never dream of being anything other than middle class as well as the many who drift slowly upwards, in that wide space between obvious 'workers' (like dockers) and obvious 'professionals' (like doctors). No doubt he is scooping in few doctors; the 4,000 or 5,000 who are in ASTMS came chiefly from a merger with the Medical Practi-tioners' Union, which left-wing G.P.s joined in the past. But Jenkins and his union have a real fascination for many profes-sional people. Gross membership has been increasing at 1,000 a week, stimulated by the publicity that ASTMS generates, as well as by full-page advertisements announcing that *My tragedy*

was I picked up a pen instead of a shovel or *I'd rather be on the
dole than join Clive Jenkins* ('It may surprise you to learn,' the
text continued, 'that Clive Jenkins understands how you feel.
He understands, but he doesn't agree.')

Jenkins says that his biggest bargaining unit consists of 8,000
people. In the event of a strike, money paid out will not be a
drain on the union's modest assets of less than half a million
pounds. He quotes figures with relish. With a headquarters cash-
flow of two million a year, which it isn't yet, but soon will be,
they could borrow up to four million from the banks, couldn't
they? Growth delights him. He thinks that perhaps two million
employees, either non-union or in weak management-dominated
bodies, are in his catchment area. City centres, full of untapped
finance and insurance companies where 'union' is a bad word,
make his eyes glitter. He is into them, just enough to whet his
appetite. He sends for daily, weekly, and monthly returns,
minutely sub-divided, fresh from the computer, and smiles
wickedly at the thought that trade unions not a million miles
away haven't the faintest idea how many members they have in
various categories. He wants more information about the firms
and jobs that ASTMS deals with. 'At the moment,' he says, 'we
are doing an awful lot of primitive, catch-as-catch-can bargaining.
I need to know what's going on.'

Jenkins is a special case, an industrial Fluellen with the gift
of tongues. But he has universal virtues. The middle classes know
his kind, though not in trade unions till now. He would be the
right man to have around in a row with the head-waiter or a
Customs officer. He is arrogant but amusing, good at stating a
case, quick to sidestep trouble. His Welsh accent is well modu-
lated, perfectly acceptable. What he says may be derisive but it
won't be offensive; it won't be crude. Since the British spend more
time listening to the way a thing is said than to the thing itself,
this puts him on firm ground. He is a palatable radical. The very
qualities that make traditional trade unionists grind their teeth
enhance his appeal to professional workers who admire achieve-
ment, whether it's his private life (such as the cottage in the
country and the cabin cruiser on the canal, now sold), or union
activity (such as cheekily recruiting alongside other unions in

banks and the Civil Service). But none of this would count for anything if Jenkins didn't have about him the air of a man who will positively deliver the goods. A professional worker can feel at home with the Jenkins style, but he can also feel reasonably confident that Jenkins will help to ensure that he is not overtaken by those ravening hordes of manual workers. The middle classes undoubtedly see themselves threatened by the bargaining power of the unions. What better answer than to achieve bargaining power of their own? 'Times have changed,' said one of the ASTMS recruiting ads. 'The old management/staff relationships have gone for ever.'

Since ASTMS is the fastest-growing union in the fastest-growing part of the movement, Jenkins is a prototype for one kind of union leader. He is successful because he understands the needs of the situation – what has to be fought for, and the best way of fighting for it. Among other things, he is a clever publicist, in a movement that is notoriously bad at communicating with the public at large. He likes writing for newspapers and making films for television (he went to North Vietnam for Thames Television in 1970). I was with him one evening when he visited London Weekend Television to see the play-back before transmission of a programme he had made in a series called 'Private Views'. He had used the programme to have a bash at some obvious targets, and do the cause of righteousness a spot of good. The big ASTMS Ford with shirt-sleeved driver had a radio-telephone that whispered and crackled to itself all the way from Camden Town to Wembley. Jenkins had invited a solicitor from the office at the last minute, laughingly. When the studio interview which formed part of the film had been recorded, there had been a little disagreement over some of the questions. Also, the original transmission had been postponed by the ITA, apparently because the programme was held to be unsuitable for the Sunday-evening slot allocated to it (eventually it went out at twenty minutes to midnight on a Saturday).

'Bill,' said Jenkins to the producer, 'this is my lawyer. Absolutely coincidental.'

'I deny I've got a writ in my pocket,' said the solicitor, also a Welshman, entering into the spirit of the thing.

In the viewing room, where the programme was to be piped through from somewhere else, the Jenkins contingent polished off nuts, crisps and gin. Apart from the lawyer and myself it included his wife, secretary, two of his children and the driver. During the usual delay in getting the film started at the other end, we talked about the protest strikes that were taking place in support of the five dockers gaoled the previous week for contempt. Jenkins said A S T M S had told its members that if they wanted to stop work as a matter of conscience, and trouble resulted when they returned, they should tell the union at once, and it would take up their case. 'We're the only union that's done that,' he said. Helping to draw the sun-blinds, drink spilt out of his glass. 'Oh, Clive *bach*!' said the solicitor.

The film got going, after two or three false starts, with Jenkins saying: 'I am forty-five years old, restless and ambitious for the people I represent. I sit on a pinnacle of institutionalized indignation.'

'Quite right,' said Jenkins from the audience.

The interviewer was Harriet Crawley. Presently she asked: 'What made you join the Communist Party?'

'I was in the Communist Party for four years, twenty years ago,' said Jenkins.

He was watching himself intently, fingers joined in front of his chest; his head, above a white shirt and dark suit, looking smaller than the solid cannonball on the screen. A clip from an Eisenstein film led him on to talk about the 'economic violence' of multinational companies – 'a danger to us all'. Over shots of London burning in the blitz he said: 'As a Welsh schoolboy during the war, I thought everyone was suffering together. I didn't realize the Dorchester and the Ritz were operating for their clientele.' After more questions about the Communist Party, Miss Crawley smiled sweetly and said: 'You have not answered a single question of mine. But never mind.' Jenkins returned an even sweeter smile. 'They were all so loaded,' he said. 'I thought I would reinterpret them for you.'

Presently he was seen talking to a group of students. 'Do you believe my thesis,' he asked one of them, 'that young people are not going to tolerate this brass-bound, stratified society?'

In the pause while the student thought about it, Jenkins hooted from the audience: 'If not, get out of my film.'

It was a good performance, on the screen and off it. His only indignation was over the questions about his days in the CP, which he regards as a distant episode; he was still grumbling to himself going off in the car. What he is now, politically, is a mellowed radical, pleased to have 150,000 members who pay the voluntary political levy to the Labour Party, highly quotable on the subject of society's inequalities, yet without the bitter doctrinaire tone of the worker-socialist. Jenkins uses his energy in a cheerful, almost light-hearted way, which suggests he is absolutely at home with the world he operates in. This isn't to say he acquiesces in its nasty capitalist ways. 'I happen to think we live in a corrupt society,' he has told journalists more than once, in identical words. 'It is busy embracing me, but I assure you the affection is not returned.' He talks about 'the capitalist jungle'. You get the feeling that his energy will continue to be spent on making the enjoyable best of it, wearing his tiger's smile. But when it comes to fighting for professional workers, his militancy is iron-hard. It would be surprising if he didn't help to crystallize existing attitudes to salary and conditions among middle-class employees, as they see the manual workers galloping closer, and make them substantially more radical over the next ten years.

The obvious weakness of white-collar unions – especially the non-technical ones – is that their bargaining power is limited because their strikes do less damage. NALGO, the National and Local Government Officers' Association, has 440,000 members, making it the fourth largest union in the country, and, it claims, the largest white-collar union in the world. Members range from typists to town clerks. 'What would happen if they went on strike?' says the general secretary, Walter Anderson. 'Well, the roads wouldn't be swept. The rates demands wouldn't go out. The libraries would close. So I suppose in a militant sense we're not strong.'

The reluctance of gentlemanly workers to stop work, thus damaging their relations with employers whose cocktail parties they might be invited to, whose positions they may even aspire to, doubtless conspires with the genuine weakness, to make it seem worse than it is. The bank clerks astonished themselves by going on strike in 1967, not for money but in order to get themselves recognized by employers who thought unions incompatible with banks. When NUBE's general secretary retired a few years later, he still sounded overwhelmed by the success of the selective strikes. 'Henry V, in his famous speech, referred to those who led at Agincourt,' he wrote in *NUBE News*. 'We too will recall names familiar in our mouths as household words ... Bolton, Blackpool, Doncaster, Nottingham ...'

The teachers were out in 1970, feeling themselves betrayed by local authorities, with women in their fifties among those who marched and waved banners. But nothing much comes grinding to a halt when schools close; there are no customers waiting for a product. 'There were a number of education authorities that balanced their budget that year,' says Edward Britton, general secretary of the NUT. 'I remember seeing one sweet young thing with a banner in London that said "Hey, hey, ILEA, How much money have you lost today?" The point was they hadn't lost anything. They'd saved her salary, and a lot of other salaries besides.' What seems to have worked in the end was the threat that teachers would refuse to supervise public examinations. But the fact that it was a real threat of real inconvenience meant that many teachers opposed it, and there were serious doubts as to whether enough of them would act. 'It brought us considerable opprobrium,' says Britton. 'For the first time, the teaching profession was subject to exactly the same expressions of horror as the power workers are when they shut down the power stations.'

Slow progress towards industrial trade unionism is not enough for groups with a Marxist flavour. NALGO has to put up with a thorn in its flesh called NAG – 'composed of a lot of youngsters who think they can put NALGO to rights overnight', says Walter Anderson. 'Their magazine calls me Lord Walter of NALGO. It's almost a schoolboyish outlook, but unfortunately it's attracted some older people who ought to know better. I kept seeing one of their activists at a conference, with a beard and faded jeans and a crumpled red pullover. I learned later that he was an economist with a nationalized industry earning *four thousand five hundred* a year.'

The NUT is pricked by a sharper goad, the Rank and File group. Teachers have always included a number of Communists, naturally enough, and party members frequently hold senior office. Rank and File's Marxists (like NAG's) are more likely to be International Socialists, opposing and opposed by the Communists. The movement claims about 2,000 subscribing members, probably has many more adherents, and achieves disproportionate publicity by staging noisy walk-outs and demonstrations at NUT conferences. It wants 'a shift of power from the minority, authoritarian position of the headmaster and education authorities, to full participation by the parents, staff, students and the community at large'. Three-quarters of the NUT executive are said to be headmasters. 'They have risen to the top of their profession so it's supposed to be natural they should rise to the top of their union,' says a Rank and File IS member. 'Cream and scum, they both rise to the surface.' The magazine, *Rank and File*, has the full range of radical reading, with more emphasis on classroom democracy than salary demands, though there are plenty of those as well. Strikes and demonstrations by pupils are generally approved of. The *Little Red School Book*, which frightened the wits out of many parents (and teachers), is described as 'excellent, if mild'.

But despite the activists, the 'middle-class' end of white-collardom remains inhibited by temperament, tradition and lack of opportunity. It is among the technicians and draughtsmen, much closer to the working class in background, that more militant steam can be generated. The leading example is TASS, formed when DATA merged with the AUEW in 1971. Its 110,000 members are concentrated in the engineering industry, with earnings from £1,500 to £5,000.

The highly militant TASS, which makes every strike by its members official, and pursues a policy of 'maximum and continuous harassment of employers', has developed from a comparatively docile union during the last ten or twelve years. Mike Cooley, a recent president, says that 'ten years ago there was a tendency to accept genteel poverty, like the teachers. We decided that we would determine unilaterally what level of wages we should get. We could then pick on individual employers and obtain settlements, and consolidate these every so often with national agreements. Having accepted the need for industrial action, our members began to use the ingenuity they have by virtue of their work. If they are capable of designing aircraft, they are capable of devising a dialectic of disrupting it. They can take hours and hours to carry out a calculation. They can look up every reference. The work is so difficult to quantify that the possibility of disruption is high.'

Cooley is one of the union's activists who changed its direction. He is a member of the China-oriented Communist Party of Great Britain (Marxist-Leninist), which has a Maoist ideology. 'It's true that our members' aspirations are of a kind to give them a political position well to the right of the leadership,' says another official. 'Most members wouldn't share the political views of the leadership. But they tolerate them.' They tolerate them because the leadership is so effective on their behalf. TASS claims to have draughtsmen of twenty-one earning £35 a week. It is also committed to looking at the future of its designers and technicians, as computer technology develops. Cooley, who writes and talks about the subject constantly, sees the strike-power of the individual in sophisticated industries increasing. He insists that this power is needed to resist a system that will put the technician at the mercy of electronic machinery, reducing him to a new drudgery in a new industrial revolution.

The alarms that Cooley sounds may be special to one kind of white-collar worker. But they have a general relevance for non-manual workers, many of whom – teachers, salesmen, journalists – may find the nature of their jobs changed out of all recognition by technology. TASS's success or otherwise in intervening in progress to its own advantage is important to others.

The next time I saw Cooley he was outside TUC House, with a contingent of TASS demonstrators who were carrying a blue and silver banner with the old words DATA embroidered in the middle. Several hundred trade unionists were lobbying the General Council, which was inside debating whether to call a general strike over the imprisoned dockers. Printers were yelling, dockers were roaring, angry slogans were bobbing up and down. I thought one or two of the TASS men looked momentarily sheepish, but there was really nothing to distinguish them from the rest.

6. Subversive Action

It is strange how little is known about 'subversive elements' in industry. A few extreme right-wing magazines and news-sheets pump out quantities of literature, frequently repetitive, full of names and too-ready inferences. A larger quantity of extreme left-wing literature establishes that an unknown proportion of trade unionists and their supporters want true socialism, and are busy trying to spread the tidings and put a quick stop to capitalism. Few ordinary people read either, and are left with brief accusations in Parliament, half-heard remarks in television programmes, and the occasional newspaper article. 'Communists infiltrate building industry,' they hear, or 'Subversives on the docks.' Statements like that mean as much or as little as anyone wants them to mean. Subversives are hardly going to explain themselves in public. So they go on being referred to or hinted at as though we all knew what was meant by them. One little difficulty for journalists is that it is libellous to call a man a Communist if he isn't one. He must be a self-confessed party member before it is safe to label him, however probable it may otherwise seem.

Subversive political militants, out to 'cause chaos' or 'topple Governments' through industrial action, are suspected not only by nervous politicians and journalists. A senior official of the TGWU, a moderate in a left-wing union, said during a 1972 dispute involving his members: 'I only wonder if some of the characters who are causing the trouble are talking for the interests of themselves, or their fellow workers – or a third party.' What would that third party be? Where was his evidence? 'I find it difficult, even with my experience. But very often, you can tell who's going to say what. When you hear something from one place, you know you're going to hear it from nine other places in twenty-four hours. That's what I mean.'

It would hardly stand up in court. But the idea of the 'outsider', the alien influence, the professional trouble-maker, is implicit in much of what is written about strikes. The role of a 'militant minority' that drags the rest of the union into a dispute it doesn't want is always news, especially since no one can prove the facts one way or the other. When the railway dispute was before the Industrial Relations Court in May 1972, it took a national ballot of railwaymen to convince the Government (which unwisely commissioned it) that nearly all of them wanted to strike. Even the mild railway clerks were two-to-one for striking. Where were the wicked militants here? A few months later, the situation was reversed, when dockers ignored their militants and went back to work. Neither case tells one much about any hard core of political activists. They may have been on the winning side with the railwaymen and the losing side with the dockers. Like God, activists work through natural causes. Grievances over pay or conditions will be there already, to be taken advantage of.

Occasionally an episode provides names and details, though never evidence. Harold Wilson, then Prime Minister, said in June 1966 that the recent seamen's strike had been aggravated by a 'tightly-knit group of politically motivated men', and named eight Communists. He said the Communist Party had used the strike not only to benefit seamen but to secure their present main objective, 'the destruction of the Government's prices and incomes policy'. The Communist Party called the allegations 'red propaganda of the most shoddy kind'. It is not that the Communists deny they are frequently involved in strikes. All they deny is that they are part of a subversive conspiracy. But is not Communism subversive by definition? The argument becomes hair-splitting.

Bert Ramelson, the Communist Party's industrial organizer, says that 'it has been quoted against me by all sorts of people, but I like to make the statement that there has not been a single mass industrial movement of any size in this country in the last decade where you don't find Communists at the centre. Let me give you a few examples. Upper Clyde Shipbuilders, with Jimmy Reid. The building industry – Pete Carter in Birmingham.

McGahey of the miners. Or take the engineering industry, wherever there's been action. There's Caborn in Sheffield, Tocher and Panter in Manchester. It's not because we stir it, but because wherever the situation develops, there you will find Communists.'

What Ramelson denies is that Communist agitators are manipulated from party headquarters in Covent Garden, behind those bullet-proof windows of greenish glass bricks. He sits in a tiny office with worn linoleum, frayed carpet and a small white bust of Lenin, explaining that situations attract activists. The scene is as a novelist with an indifferent imagination who had never been inside Communist Party headquarters might picture it. Ramelson is in his early sixties, a former barrister, a Canadian, born in the Ukraine; he says 'arction' and 'farctory'. He describes his job as firstly to advise the party, secondly to help frame policy for different industries. But this is not manipulation. 'Like-minded people get together – but that is a different matter from my directing, isn't it? The idea that there is a conspiracy, and I sit here deciding what people will run for what jobs, is totally wrong. When you use words like "Communist-dominated", I feel this is almost insulting to the British worker. It suggests they are simpletons, allowing a tiny minority to dominate them. If the Communist Party were not saying what the workers felt, they would be ignored. They make proposals which are not totally removed from reality.'

He simplifies things, presumably for my benefit. 'Our motive is to undermine capitalism. We make no bones about it. People are living in an illusory world. If you remove the sand from the ostrich, he sees the sun. If this is cataclysmic, well, fine.' A poster on the wall shows blood coming from a squeezed figure, with the caption 'Crush anti-union laws'. Strikes to achieve political ends, such as having the Industrial Relations Act repealed, are welcome to the Communists, who find themselves riding the wave of protest over the Act that has put Communists and moderates in the same loose alliance. Ramelson says the trade union movement is 'more militant than at any time in its history, not excluding the General Strike, or 1911 and 1912. Simultaneously, the party's influence on policy, on strategy and on using the confidence of members to elect Communists is higher than ever in the history of the party.'

To Ramelson, then, it is a question of 'influence'. The word is safely non-committal. Once you begin to look for 'influence' rather than 'manipulation', it lies all around. The national executive of the Communist Party has forty-two members, at least twenty-five of them trade unionists. One third of these are from a single union, the A U E W. Eddie Marsden is general secretary of the union's Constructional Section. One of the shop-floor engineers is Dick Etheridge, convenor at British Leyland's Longbridge plant. George Wake, who works in a power station, leads the Power Worker group of militants. John Tocher of Manchester is there, and so is Jimmy Reid of Upper Clyde, and Michael McGahey, the miners' president in Scotland. Other members belong to the T G W U, N A L G O, the National Union of Public Employees, the agricultural workers, the seamen's union and a printing union, S O G A T. Naturally they don't see themselves as trouble-makers. Wake says briskly: 'You can't have a conspiracy on the shop-floor. I'd say that in the electricity supply industry, I've stopped more disputes than I've caused.' Etheridge, a heavy, even-tempered man, says that 'the reality of negotiating is that conflict is endemic to the system. This isn't a bad thing, provided it's channelled to useful purpose. But if it means that one side or the other has to go to the wall, you have a dialogue and compromise on it.' Etheridge distinguishes carefully between Communists and other, more militant militants, like the Trotskyists. Discussing payment systems in the motor industry,* he says: 'I don't regard a wages system as a principle. The Trots do, silly buggers. But you've got to have some system. Communist countries use measured day-work, come to that. I'd regard my job as to get the best possible deal, whatever the system. If you're asking what system is the best, I'd say piecework, but if it comes to having a confrontation and smashing the whole thing up, I'd say no. But the Trots do. They're the ones who want to create the conditions that create chaos.'

Whatever the influence of Communists, it is obviously greater if they are well placed in industry. But Ramelson will deride the

*See Chapter 4, p. 53.

idea that Jimmy Reid, for instance, was moved in to Upper Clyde, ready for the drama of the work-in when the yard went into liquidation. 'Communists never "move in". He was in engineering when we asked him to be a full-time worker for the party. But eventually he reached a position where he found it difficult to live on a party wage. So he went back to work, to the industry he knew. He wouldn't want to lock himself up in a little rat-shop with ten people. But who could have said three or four years ago that U C S was a place where things would blow up as they did?'

I had a mildly informative conversation with Neil Milligan, London organiser of A S L E F, the engine-drivers' union. An article in *The Times** had suggested that the fact that the railway dispute was at its worst in the Southern Region might not be unconnected with the fact that Milligan, based at Waterloo, was an active Communist. Milligan, a Scotsman, had moved to London from Scotland with his family in January 1972, when the railway negotiations were warming up. I asked him if it would be foolish to see the move as politically motivated. No, he said, it wouldn't be foolish. But it was difficult. The move was nothing to do with the union, for a start. Among the reasons were personal reasons. But it wasn't easy to give an honest answer to the question. We sat staring into our drinks in the station buffet at Waterloo, and I said: 'What do we do, then, leave the question on the table?' Milligan smiled broadly. 'As Robbie Burns said, we'll let that fly stick to the wall.'

Anyone who looks for Communists among shop stewards or union officials will soon find them, often in important posts. It is not their job to take a back seat. The little cluster of three officials in the Manchester region is in a key position. So is Etheridge at Longbridge, where about twenty of the stewards are Communists (together with half a dozen other Marxists), out of the total of 750. Proportionate to countrywide Communist membership, the number of stewards would be nearer two. But there is no mystery about it. Communists want to get elected; most trade unionists don't. They are voted in and they can be voted out. According to Aidan Crawley, 'at least 10 per cent of the senior posts in our major industrial unions are held

*'Communist influence on industrial strife', Nigel Lawson, 24 May 1972

by Communists or open sympathisers'.* If true, this should surprise no one. Communists sit on the executives of the National Union of Teachers, the National Union of Miners, the A U E W, A S L E F and many more. They are there at least partly because the Communists care about union activities and most of their brothers don't. Union apathy has been much criticized. Frank Chapple, moderate leader of the electricians and plumbers, says that 'you hear people talk about "what the workers think", but when you go along to a meeting, you'll find about six of the workers there – two Communists, two Maoists and two Labour councillors.'

The best documented case of Communists in key posts was the E T U affair in 1961;† unfortunately for the party it is also the best documented case of trade union chicanery, enabling endless references back whenever the subject of 'Communist manipulation' is raised. In his summing up, Mr Justice Winn remarked that although Communists accounted for only about 1 per cent of the union's members, they held the posts of president, general secretary, assistant general secretary, and five of the executive council seats. The official who ran the London area was a Communist, and so were eight of its ten sub-committee members. The lawsuit concerned only one post, that of general secretary. But the outcome rubbed off on Communists holding union office in general.

A few busy Marxists will influence a situation in perfectly legal ways. Dick Etheridge thinks there are no more than six Trotskyist shop stewards at Longbridge, but 'they can create a bother, especially in the present climate'. Mike Cooley of T A S S, the Maoist, wrote an illuminating article for *Rank and File*, the teachers' Marxist magazine, in which he said that

the membership of my union did not wake up one morning all realizing that they had to oppose the Industrial Relations Act. There was no spontaneity about it. It was based on a vigorous campaign waged by the leadership and the activists of the union ... Weekend schools were held all over the country ... almost every one of our 250 branches held several meetings ... a special summer school was held at Ruskin College ... The union spent thousands on the campaign.

*The *Financial Times*, 8 March 1972.
†See Chapter 4, page 49.

The response of the radical left to the Industrial Relations Act offers the best recent example of trade-union strength being harnessed for a political end. The Communists have rarely had such a popular trade-union cause to advocate. Opposition has been organized around the Liaison Committee for the Defence of Trade Unions, set up in 1966 to oppose the growing movement to curb union militants by some form of legislation. It has organized conferences and demonstrations, and has acted as an effective focus for opposition, first to the Labour Government's 'In Place of Strife', later to the Conservatives' Act. Up to a thousand delegates, mainly from union branches and shop stewards' committees, have attended conferences. The chairman and secretary, Kevin Halpin and Jim Hiles, are both Communists, and party members are prominent on the platform. The liaison committee has become increasingly acceptable to unions as the movement has drifted leftwards.

Many non-Communists approve of it. But right-wing observers see it, as a matter of course, as set up and managed by the Communist Party. Ramelson denies it is managed in any sense, and again stresses 'influence' as opposed to 'manipulation'. The committee, he says, 'arose following the discussions that began to take place in the Labour Government in 1964, about introducing legislation to interfere with union negotiating. Militant shop stewards saw this as the thin end of the wedge. Two or three of them took the initiative by writing to fifty or sixty leading factories. Those that responded became the sponsors. They held a series of discussions and action conferences, and succeeded in making the movement aware of the threat. There were industrial stoppages, the T U C began to react, and it certainly led to the T U C's own campaign against the Act. It is a genuine rank-and-file movement, with Communists to the fore.'

Well organized and with strong party discipline, the Communists remain the most effective group of militants who would use industrial action for political ends. But they seek formal political power through the normal electoral process; they still hope that one day, light will dawn on the people, who will vote them into Parliament. Beyond the Communists are the less patient revolutionaries. The Trotskyists, organized chiefly in the Socialist

Labour League, are the most prominent, opposed to compromise of any kind with capitalism or parliamentary democracy. Their industrial organization is the All Trades Union Alliance. The other main Marxist faction is International Socialists, a group which originated in the 1950s as a Trotskyist breakaway, impugning the Soviet system as 'State capitalist'. IS speaks in a less fanatical voice than the Trotskyists, but is no less anxious to change society. It seeks to 'build a revolutionary workers' party in Britain'. Both groups circulate large amounts of literature. *Socialist Worker*, the weekly IS newspaper, has extensive industrial coverage, favouring rank-and-file movements (where it is well informed), and is more likely to use its invective against trade-union leaders, who obstinately insist on cooperating with the State, than to waste it on employers. According to one of its small staff, two unions, the TGWU and GMWU, even refuse to put it on their mailing list for literature. The offset-litho printing shop in Shoreditch produces other militant newspapers, among them that of the NALGO ginger group, NAG, and the *Carworker*, a 'rank-and-file paper run by and for motor vehicle and component workers', which takes a straightforward IS line, inasmuch as any fringe-Marxist line is capable of being straightforward. Teaching, local government, the car industry and engineering are among the areas where IS seems comparatively well represented. According to the right-wing eagles, Fleet Street and television have also been 'penetrated'. Since IS is the freshest-looking and least depressing brand of revolutionary socialism on offer at the moment, it would be surprising if it didn't have adherents in the media.

In industry generally, employers are sometimes heard to say that the Communists aren't so bad – 'you know where you are with the Comms' – and that the Trots and International Socialists now cause the headaches. This is probably a reaction to local unofficial tactics, where the fringe groups are often more active than the Communists, who keep their energy for broader strategies. British Leyland groans at Trotskyist activities in parts of the Cowley plant, where about half a dozen Marxist shop stewards are regarded as 'troublemakers', though rarely referred to as such in public. 'I would think that most members of the

Communist Party have the improvement of the working class
as their basic need', said one of the managers there. 'Most of the
revolutionary Marxists have moved away, to I S or the Socialist
Labour League.'

The Communists themselves loathe the other groups as rivals,
a sentiment that merges into the working man's resentment at
clever fellows from outside who tell him what his attitude to work
should be. Dick Etheridge says darkly that he would like to know
where the money comes from for *Socialist Worker* and *Carworker*,
because he never sees anyone buying them at Longbridge.
'They come down to the factory gates and try to tell us what to do.
Bugger it, they're patronizing.' An old-style branch official in
Yorkshire, responding suspiciously to my questions over the
telephone about a strike I had read about in *Socialist Worker*,
advised me to tread warily when reading 'a very left-wing
reactionary newspaper like that'. He wouldn't put much credence
in it himself. 'Nay,' he said, 'it's not a trade-union newspaper.
It's run by *university students*.'

For those who wish to have their blood chilled by accounts of
what subversive elements are up to, there is an extensive esoteric
literature. It is characteristic of Britain that instead of political
militants in industry being a subject for regular, straightforward
inquiry and discussion, nobody bothers much except for these
small right-wing groups; and the way in which they bother has
undertones of witch-hunting. A steady flow of material appears in
East-West Digest, a bi-monthly magazine at £5 a year, edited by a
Conservative MP, Geoffrey Stewart-Smith, supported by a group
concerned about subversion – no names available over the
telephone – and put out by the Foreign Affairs Publishing Co.
The *Digest* commonly has three or four articles about Marxists
in different parts of industry. Their message is simple: the
enemy is at the gates. Regular features include one headed
'Parliament' which shows a drawing of the House of Commons
exploding and Big Ben falling to the ground. Among other
organizations, Common Cause is a small affair that issues a thin
stream of warning literature, some of it about Marxists in
industry. I R I S, Industrial Research and Information Services,
which operates from a terraced house near the Oval, began as an

offshoot of Common Cause, and now provides a service for unions and others who want to see the world through the eyes of a right-wing trade unionist. Andy McKeown, who runs it, is a Roman Catholic who believes that 'if you get informed trade unionists, there is no hope for the Communists'.

Most interesting of all is the Economic League, set up after the First World War by industrialists who feared the revolution, which provides a sophisticated information service about industrial relations in general and subversives in particular. Much of its information is culled from left-wing literature, but it also has its own contacts, which it prefers to say nothing about, except that they are 'trade unionists who feel as strongly as we do about the activities of subversives in their unions'. Industrial companies pay a regular subscription or make donations. In return they are supplied with information about militants. The League insists that services like this are only a small part of its work. But they are the part that many of the clients want. What they receive may be no more than a few names and a brief linking-up of incidents in which militants have been involved, but it helps to provide a background. A leading motor manufacturer once told me (1969) that the League 'does a hell of a lot of security vetting for us on political grounds'.

Industry as seen from right-wing vantage points has a glowing pattern of subversion under its surface. The Comms, the Trots, the liaison committees, glow brightest of all. Faint lines connect the centres to the periphery. The Institute for Workers' Control, a favourite subject with the *East-West Digest*, is included for its Marxist connections. An information service concentrating on industrial and union matters, the Labour Research Department, which was proscribed by the Labour Party until 1972, is in the picture. The *Digest* obligingly lists numerous Communists on its executive and staff. There is the *Voice* series of newspapers, in particular *Engineering Voice*. According to 'The Agitators', an Economic League booklet, Communist-influenced conferences organized by *Engineering Voice* provided much of the support that helped to get Hugh Scanlon and other left-wing candidates elected to AUEW posts in the late 1960s. There is no suggestion it was improper: only that it was skilful.

Somewhere in the pattern is the pale hint of sabotage in industry. A 1971 issue of *Solidarity*, a magazine produced by a group of that name, speaks kindly of sabotage and gives helpful information about

neglecting to maintain or lubricate machinery at the correct intervals, pushing buttons on complex electronic gear in the wrong order, putting pieces in the wrong way, running machines at the wrong speeds or feeds, dropping foreign bodies in gear boxes, 'technological indiscipline': each industry and trade has its established practices, its own traditions.

It suggests that sabotage has a 'long and honourable history', and shrewdly sees the reality as being

both less sensational and more significant than the myth. Sabotage is essentially a part of the informal resistance. It usually takes the form of individual actions. Taken altogether it is undoubtedly a significant form of struggle.

The argument is that the bosses are getting at the workers, so the workers will get at the bosses. An earlier issue of *Solidarity* (1964) contained an article about Ford Motors at Dagenham:

The cry of 'Stop fucking about!' could be the theme song at Fords. I once saw a new man stop work to blow his nose. While he fumbled for his handkerchief the charge-hand rushed up. 'What's wrong, has the machine broken?'

'No, I'm just blowing my nose,' the man answered.

'Well, you're not paid to blow your nose,' screamed the charge-hand. 'You're paid to work. Don't let me see you fucking about again!'

The underground newspaper *Ink*, now defunct, printed a three-page feature headed 'Spanners in the works' (17 December 1971) which extolled the virtues of sabotage ('Creative vandalism is the life-blood of a mass movement') and reported various incidents, including half a mile of Blackpool rock produced with the message 'Fuck off'. This sounds apocryphal, like the nineteenth century story, told of *The Times* and other newspapers, about the printer under notice who inserted an obscene sentence in the middle of a Parliamentary report. But, true or false, the spirit is recognizable.

The key to sabotage is in the *Solidarity* phrases, 'informal resistance' and 'individual actions'. There is no evidence that it is more widespread than in the past. Managements prefer not to discuss it. 'There are occasionally suspicions,' says a motor manufacturer, 'but if the company goes on record as suggesting it's even possible, the cry goes up that you're trying to malign honest workers. But if your labour relations go wrong, your quality goes off. Then you get to a point where vehicles have to be re-worked because the inspectors are picking up more than average minor defects.'

The reality of 'subversion' is not men plotting to blow up factories, any more than it is tight-knit political networks following master strategies to incite the peace-loving workers. It is rather the harnessing of discontents, sometimes on a large scale, often locally and at short notice, by political radicals. The discontents come first. The significant change of the last few years has been the way they have increased – grievances about pay, about the worker's share in industry, about the Industrial Relations Act. The discontents have the radicals in tow, not the other way round. But, having had their base widened for them, the professional militants have deliberately widened it further. The unions didn't need the Liaison Committee for the Defence of Trade Unions to make them object to 'In Place of Strife' and the Industrial Relations Act, but it is reasonable to think that the committee sharpened the edge of protest. The union movement was swinging to the left through the sixties in response to fundamental changes of mood; Hugh Scanlon might have been elected if no one had lifted a finger to help him. But because he was the best left-wing candidate it was practical to get elected, the Communists and other radicals supported him, and presumably helped to shift opinion in his favour. The usual small minority actually voted – around 12 per cent in the second of two ballots that elected him. There was nothing subversive about the end product: a man who had never made any secret of his views had been democratically chosen to lead a union. But a party bent on replacing the 'illusory world' of capitalism had done its share.

Perhaps this is why the subject is so under-reported. It defies analysis except in partisan terms. It has to be argued, not reported. Subversion is ideas.

7. Signals at Red

Railwaymen are not among nature's militants. 'The railways' traditionally mean steady jobs for steady fellows, though for substantially fewer fellows in recent years, as the industry contracts. Sir Sidney Greene, general secretary of the National Union of Railwaymen (198,000 members), is every politician's idea of what a union leader should be. He wears sober suits and is inclined to lapse in public into a solemn trade-union jargon, like an echo of a conference at Blackpool or Brighton. Percy Coldrick, general secretary of the Transport Salaried Staffs Association, the white-collar workers (75,000), is a stately figure. The nearest to a railway militant is Ray Buckton, general secretary of the small Associated Society of Locomotive Engineers and Firemen (29,000), the train drivers' union. Buckton is a blunter man with a harsher turn of phrase, leading a union of skilled craftsmen, jealous of their rights, aware of their power to stop the railways.

The three unions sought a pay rise in 1972, and took industrial action when the Government wouldn't give them what they asked. They were angrier and more demanding than usual. The miners, fellow workers in another nationalized industry, had recently compelled the Government to settle on the union's terms. The railwaymen were anxious to copy the miners, and the Government was equally anxious to stop them. Trouble of some kind was likely.

What distorted the simple conflict was the Government's decision to use its new Industrial Relations Act in an attempt to slow down events. The Act, the most controversial piece of domestic legislation for many years, was already in tentative use over a dispute involving Liverpool dockers. It had been invoked by a road-haulage firm against shop stewards who were blacking its lorries. A different section of the Act was now invoked by the Government. Like a new-model fire-engine, hitherto untried against real flames, it emerged from the Government garage, lights rotating, siren moaning, firemen thumbing hastily through the maker's instructions to see how the pumps worked. Greene, Coldrick and Buckton watched in amazement as this machine whizzed into sight, and set about dousing their humble blaze. In no time the flames were twice as high. Petrol, perhaps, was coming from the hoses instead of water. The new-model fire-engine retreated, paintwork badly blistered, and the conflagration burnt itself out in the usual way. As a machine it had considerable merit, but its first full-scale exercise hardly inspired confidence. In public, Greene, Coldrick and Buckton wore pained expressions. But in private, when it was over, and they had what they wanted, they were grinning.

The Industrial Relations Act was an attempt to regulate the balance of power between unions and State. It is still relatively untried, and if its use had developed in the leisurely way that the Government implied while it was being debated, Act and unions might have had time to mould their surfaces to fit one another. But some politicians and employers itched to use the dangerous clauses, their desire to curb the unions increased by the violence of union opposition to the prospect of a law that made them more accountable for their actions. The campaign to 'Kill the Bill' had confirmed that the unions intended nothing to change. This was the kind of behaviour that the advocates of the Bill objected to. The unions spoke of 'self-defence'; the title of the coordinating left-wing group, the Liaison Committee for the Defence of Trade Unions, incorporated the idea. But did the unions need defending against the State, or was it the other way round? Militants on both sides wanted to force the issue as soon as possible.

Historically, unions had been persecuted for organizing strikes. Over the years a series of laws protected them, as employers sought fresh loopholes in existing laws. The emphasis lay on safeguarding the unions when they were weak. There was no specific provision for controlling them as they became stronger. After 1945 they arrived at a situation where militants would strike 'unofficially', as and when it suited them. The curbs of poverty and starvation had lost their old stringency; so had the working man's inherited sense of defeat. A complex way of life, the interlocking of industries and services, made employers and public more vulnerable. Relatively, the workers had increased their power. In practice, almost any strike was legal. In the 1950s, right-wing unions objected to having their powers usurped by the rank and file. But this objection faded as unions shifted to the left, making rank-and-file action more acceptable, and also producing more 'official' militancy from the top.

The containment of strikes was the most important single object of the Industrial Relations Act, which grew out of 'A Giant's Strength', the Donovan Report and twenty years of realizing that the workers had changed. Under the Act, unions were well advised (though not compelled) to apply for registration. If they did not register, any strike by them or their members exposed them to the risk of legal action; they also lost exemption from income tax on investments, which could cost a large union a million pounds or more in a year. If they did register, their rule books, elections and discipline had to be approved by a registrar. Once registered, a union could call a strike as long as it didn't fall into a new category created by the Act, the unfair industrial practice. To a militant trade unionist, the U I P was too bad to be true. All unofficial strikes were unfair. So were all sympathetic strikes by one union in support of another. So was action that induced a party to a contract to break it. Redress could be sought by an employer at N I R C, the National Industrial Relations Court, set up under the Act to hear (among other things) complaints about unfair practices. Such a complaint couldn't be about strikers in general, but had to be directed at the union or the unofficial strike leaders.

The other direct sanction against strikes was contained in a procedure for the State to use in a national emergency. The Government could apply to the court for a cooling-off period of up to sixty days, and a secret ballot if the workers were thought to be less enthusiastic than their leaders alleged. This was regarded by most pundits as a last resort, unlikely to be used until Britain was sinking under waves of chaos.

The Act introduced the law, for the first time, into the question of whether or not a worker should belong to a union. With certain qualifications, it left him free to decide, and made pressure from the union illegal. Other provisions were designed to protect worker against employer, for instance in case of unfair dismissal. Much of the Act dealt with conciliation. It was possible to present the entire measure as a 'new framework for industrial relations'. The Central Office of Information's official summary of the provisions began with 'Rights of Workers' and didn't reach 'Unfair Industrial Practices' for a page and a half. But to most unions, the Act, if not death, was a major calamity. To shop stewards and any who wanted the freedom to strike as they pleased, it meant the end of an era. The likely effect of the Act would be to subordinate them to the official leadership of the union, which in turn now had to operate within a precise legal framework. The question of 'Who runs a union?' would be decisively settled in favour of union headquarters.

In the winter and early spring, while the Act was still a presence behind the scenes, the railwaymen were busy negotiating. These sessions are unwieldy affairs, with thirty or forty executive members and senior officers from the union side, facing a smaller group from the Railways Board. What the unions wanted was an increase of 14 per cent (or 16 per cent for locomotive-men, calculated on a different basis) on average earnings of £35 for a driver and £28 for station staff, with overtime included. Buckton originally wanted half as much again. He says regretfully that he was already using the phrase 'a special case' to describe the train drivers when the miners pre-empted it in February. But the railway unions watch one another like hawks. 'Sid Greene made it very clear that if we got twenty per cent, he'd want twenty per cent too,' says Buckton. 'So we had to come off what we were arguing, which in fact was twenty-five per cent, and drop to sixteen, which we all agreed.'

Negotiations had been going on since the previous November, without the Railways Board making an offer. One rule of the game is to put off naming a figure as long as possible. The Board observed gloomily that when they met the unions the week after the miners' award, the railwaymen carried copies of the Wilberforce Report. Paragraph 30 of the report caused particular gloom; it spoke of the Government having to find the money, a course which the Board had been insisting was not possible. According to the Board, no one had any money, or at least no one had 14 per cent.

Bargaining began with an offer of 8 per cent on 6 March. By the end of the month the figure had risen to 11. There is evidence that the Board would have been slower and meaner but for the urgent need to restock power stations with coal after the miners' strike. A settlement was needed. But at 11 per cent, it was the unions' turn. Greene, Coldrick and Buckton would slide gently down the slope and meet the Board halfway. But they never did. The unions clung to their original figure. Even when an arbitrator, Alex Jarratt, was brought in one weekend by mutual agreement, and emerged from silent meditation on Sunday evening to announce a Solomon's judgement worth $12\frac{1}{2}$ per cent, the unions refused to compromise. The Board was astonished. One of them said afterwards that it was like wrestling with a jelly. The unions were equally astonished, or so they still insist. They thought Mr Jarratt the arbitrator was a painless device to let them have their money without anyone losing face. 'That's what arbitration is, passing the buck,' says Greene. 'Our understanding was that the Board didn't want an arbitrator, they wanted a conciliator who would tell the Government what it must pay', says Coldrick. 'I was honestly to God led to believe that it only needed an independent person to open that door,' says Buckton. Perhaps the unions deluded themselves because they sensed and were influenced by a new mood among their members – though Greene admits he knew that many of his men didn't want to strike at first. Buckton's militants were stirring. At Waterloo Station, footplatemen would explain, to journalists who always seemed to lack space to print all they had to say, that they were more militant there because drivers earned less in mileage bonuses for short journeys round the suburbs – 'All you see is chimbley pots and back gardens.' Or they would make huge melancholy generalizations, like 'The driver lost his authority when the steam engine went,' and explain patiently why diesels were anonymous, incomprehensible machines. Derrick Fullick, from a family of train-drivers, would say, 'You hear more political discussions now than you ever heard on the railway. A year ago I was a political moron.' Neil Milligan, ASLEF organizer, would say, with Marxist presumption, 'Derrick can drive a train into London at ten to nine with maybe seven millionaires on board – no, correction, they don't come in till half past ten or eleven. The railwaymen are beginning to say, what is our contribution to society? What's theirs?'

The Government is said to have decided to use the Industrial Relations Act, should the situation warrant it, at a Cabinet meeting on 13 April. At that point the pay talks were in deadlock, the unions were threatening to ban overtime and to work to rule, and some train crews on the Southern Region were already disrupting services. When Jarratt's compromise was rejected a few days later, a full work-to-rule followed from midnight on the Sunday, 16 April. On Wednesday afternoon, the Government applied to the Industrial Relations Court for a cooling-off period, and the new-model fire-engine was launched on its mission.

Relations between the two sides were already less than cordial. The unions had been unhappy about the flavour of the negotiations, sensing (they claimed) that the hand of the Government was visible more than usual. In theory nationalized industries negotiate independently; in practice they are subject to obvious pressures. 'There was too much going out of the room by the Board negotiators,' says Buckton. 'Not the usual, I've-got-to-ask-me-Dad.' It was widely suggested that the Prime Minister, defeated by the miners, meant to teach the railwaymen a lesson. A senior Minister, Anthony Barber, spoke of 'blackmail by sectional groups seeking their own self-interest'. Tempers rose further when the Secretary for Employment, the newly appointed Maurice Macmillan, warned the unions the day after the Jarratt arbitration failed that the Act was about to be used. Trade unions are always touchy; the Act made them touchier still. Greene let it be known that Macmillan had marched out 'clicking his heels, without a goodbye, kiss-my-arse or thank you'. Next day

Greene arrived precisely one hour late for further talks with the Minister, remarking that he was not accustomed to receiving 'a thump around the flippin' earhole'.

When the Government's application went before the industrial court, the unions were not represented. This was in keeping with the TUC's policy of non-cooperation. Unions had been told to remain off the register, and most had done so. Collectively the movement seems to have felt that if it turned its back on the Act, the legislation would mysteriously lose its power. Reality intervened that third Wednesday in April in the shape of telephone calls between offices, and clerks in taxis delivering letters by hand. The Government's application arrived at the court just before lunch. Soon letters had gone out to the unions, advising them of the hearing at 4 p.m. The man who went to ASLEF had a longer journey because the union is outside central London, in South Hampstead. Its bare, polished entrance hall is like a first-class waiting room from a railway station in the great days of steam. 'He walked in,' says Buckton, 'and he said, "Are you Raymond Buckton?" "I am", I said. "Are you the general secretary of the Associated Society of Locomotive Engineers and Firemen?" I said, "I wouldn't be sat here if I wasn't." Then I drew back. I just sat tapping the desk. He handed me the letter and I said, "I will see my lawyer." He said, "I am employed by the National Industrial Relations Court. Good afternoon." But it was all the wrong atmosphere for industrial relations.'

The court had to decide whether the railwaymen's work-to-rule was an 'irregular industrial action' within the meaning of the Act, and whether it was doing grave damage to the economy. The unions hoped that their old hair-splitting argument, that by following the rule book literally they were merely being punctilious, would prevail. Its chances would have been small even if union barristers had been present, and it was quickly disposed of. A threat to the economy was accepted, and the court ordered a cooling-off period of fourteen days, seven days less than the Government had requested. Any thoughts the railway unions might have had about defying the court were abruptly ended next day, when the court's £5,000 fine on the TGWU in the lorry-blacking case was increased by £50,000 because the blacking had not been stopped. Orders went out to end the work-to-rule, and an uneasy peace followed for the next fortnight.

Nothing much happened. Unions and Railways Board thought of talking in seclusion, away from the pressures of London. Someone suggested Watford Junction; someone else, more inspired but less practical, proposed they cruise in the North Sea on board a railway ferry. The Board wanted to prise union leaders away from the stony ranks of colleagues, among them Communist colleagues, sitting behind them at the talks. Eventually this was achieved at some sessions. But when the negotiators did talk, they continued to disagree and misunderstand one another. The Board's offer went up a bit. The haggling now, it seemed, was about whether the increase should be paid from 1 May or 1 June. This tiny enclave was all the Government had left to fight for.

The railway militants grumbled that their leaders should not have cooperated with the court. *Private Eye* made jokes about the arrest of British Railways ('18,426 miles of track, 15,688 engines, three sepia views of Dorset beauty-spots'). There were militants who would have welcomed open conflict. According to Buckton, the A S L E F executive originally decided it would not call off the work-to-rule, and changed its mind only to conform with the N U R and T S S A. There was more anger still when the cooling-off period ended without agreement, and four days later, on 12 May, as rail services around London became chaotic again, the Government used the other prong of the Act's emergency procedure, and applied for a ballot of railwaymen. The court agreed to it, and once again the work-to-rule was supposed to pause. But the unions, belatedly recognising the Act's existence, took the decision to the Court of Appeal, which sat hurriedly to hear the arguments, while trains ran late or didn't run at all, and commuters brandished umbrellas at locomotive-men. Trains out of Victoria, Waterloo and other Southern Region stations stopped during the evening rush-hour on 15 May, and passengers made angry scenes of their own.

Derrick Fullick says that 'one of the men phoned me and said I'd better get to the depot because we were going to have a close-down, so I jumped in the car and came to Waterloo. The newspapers said it was about a foreman that got taken off, but it wouldn't have mattered what it was, the lads were looking for an excuse to say, Up your pipe. That sort of thing's never occurred in this industry. The footplatemen used to be puddings. Militant? Who are you comparing them with? Other railwaymen? Not with the dockers, anyway. Not with the car workers. But it's surprising how quickly you can educate yourself.'

Buckton says that before the Act was used, there were 'big areas' of ASLEF, let alone the other two unions, that didn't want industrial action. Things changed quickly, with the Waterloo depot in the lead. 'I knew what was happening at Waterloo. I knew they were taking unofficial action, and I had my own views about it. Mac[millan] thought we had lost control, but what does "control" mean, in a voluntary organization? What do you do in a trade union? Get them by the scruff of the neck and say, "Work that train"?'

It was the nearest the railways came to the question of 'Who runs a union?', smouldering away at the core of the Act. In a different shape, the dilemma had already cost the TGWU £55,000 in fines for the behaviour of shop stewards in Liverpool. On the railways, the issue loomed up vaguely and went away again. The situation was too confused, with lawyers arguing and negotiators wrangling. Train services wobbled and returned more or less to normal. The appeal court decided the ballot was in order, and voting forms were dispatched to railwaymen, not without confusion, for them to indicate with an X whether they did or didn't wish to take part in further industrial action. A humorous note was introduced by rumours that the Government was sitting on the report of its Review Body on Top Salaries, thinking it not quite the time to announce that the pay of Richard Marsh at the Railways Board was to go up from £20,000 to £22,500.*

Then the result of the ballot was announced. It was better than the unions could have hoped for, worse than the Government could have feared. Greene's station staff voted 80,000 for industrial action, only 10,000 against. Buckton's drivers had an

---

*The report was published the following month, accompanied by Lobby briefings for political correspondents which pointed out that the increases were patriotically small when viewed as a percentage. Workers earning £1,500 a year no doubt had their own view of a £2,500 increase.

overwhelming 23,000 for and 1,000 against. Even the clerks and executives of TSSA voted 21,000 to 10,000.* The clerks were amazed at their temerity; so were other union leaders. The ballot drew white-collar railwaymen and uniformed workers closer. It showed how far militancy had seeped through the three unions. 'The ordinary engine-driver gets to Grantham,' says Buckton, 'and he looks in his newspaper and he sees his union has been accused of blackmail. Well, he's going to vote for the people he pays his money to. He'd be a fool if he didn't, wouldn't he?'

The Act had done nothing to lower the temperature; it had done the reverse. It was true that the unions had been forced to recognize the court, by briefing barristers to attend it. Certain ground-rules for future situations had been established, notably that a work-to-rule could constitute a breach of contract; the decision by Donaldson was upheld by the appeal court, though overtime working, it seemed, could be legitimately withdrawn by unions. No doubt the first sessions of the court were bound to contain tentative and controversial rulings, raw bones for the lawyers to gnaw. But the intention, if one listened to the politicians beforehand, had not been to let loose a stream of decisions whose immediate effect was to exacerbate the situations they dealt with. Yet it may have been what angry men on both sides secretly wanted.

A by-product of the court's intervention was alarm at the effect NIRC might have on the reporting and debating of industrial disputes. This issue was left in the air for another occasion. At least two 'friendly' telephone calls were made by the court to the BBC following programmes. One of the programmes had contained a possibly irreverent description of NIRC. The other showed railwaymen at Waterloo declaring they had no intention of obeying the court. As a result, programme editors were advised of a legal risk in allowing speakers to preach defiance. Unrest in Fleet Street led to a statement from Donaldson on 8 June designed to allay fears. *The Times* headline, 'Press May

*The numbers voting were well below union membership. Many rail-union members work outside the railways, or were otherwise not entitled to vote – e.g. those in workshops or in management grades.

Comment Responsibly on Industrial Court', summed up its intent; the words 'responsible' and 'responsibility' occurred four times in the statement. On the same day Donaldson gave a private briefing to industrial correspondents. These occasions, like the invidious Lobby meetings for political journalists, are not supposed to be directly referred to afterwards. But this meeting was allegedly described some weeks later in an article in *Socialist Worker*, which gave an account of the briefing that made the court's attitude sound sterner. The account was detailed (is there an International Socialist among industrial reporters?). It said that Donaldson 'made it quite clear that the press should not only refrain from supporting workers taking direct action, but should not quote workers' leaders in such a way that their words might encourage other workers to take direct action'. Private reports of this private briefing, which officially didn't take place, are confused. But journalists are left uneasy about possible pitfalls in reporting future episodes. Months later the BBC was still discussing internally what its attitude should be.

After the fiasco of the ballot, the negotiations stumbled into their final phase. First came a week of further deadlock, with Coldrick restraining his colleagues from re-imposing the overtime ban. Finally the Railways Board agreed to a formula that would give the unions the last couple of million pounds they wanted. The negotiators shook the paper-clips out of their briefcases. Greene said it was satisfactory. So did Coldrick. Buckton called it a great victory. As the most militant of the three union leaders, he received the usual offerings from the unknown public: a commuter's ruined dinner in a cardboard box with a letter from the wife; parcels of books he had never ordered; visits from insurance salesmen he had never requested; soiled lavatory paper and other obscenities.

Down at Waterloo, in their mess room above the platforms, the locomotive men made tea and hot sandwiches, and said they were more socialistic than most depots, but not really political. Drivers' caps and jackets with leather elbows hung on pegs along the shiny yellow wall. A telephone clamped alongside rang intermittently with requests for crews. Derrick Fullick said he had been to a meeting of the Liaison Committee for the Defence of Trade Unions; he had been sent an invitation. 'It's supposed to be Communist-dominated,' he said, 'but I found that the shop stewards were not the fanatics I had imagined them to be. The line put out by the chairman wasn't that people like myself should form minority groups, but they should fall in line behind trade-union leaders and show them what the rank and file felt. I expected a lot of long-haired weirdies getting up and advocating revolution, but I could see what they were doing. They weren't preaching revolution. They were trying to convey a message to the unions.'

A driver with grey hair an inch long complained that, as usual, the public thought the workers had been awarded more than they had been. The locomotive men were reported as getting an extra £5, but £1.80 of this was at the expense of mileage bonuses, so the true figure was £3.20, and as a matter of fact, a month after the settlement, they still hadn't actually seen it. The computer was to blame. 'It used to be old Jim next door,' somebody said. 'He never made a mistake or, if he did, it was always to overpay you.'

A driver with black shoulder-length hair, gold rings on two fingers and a gold locket on a chain around his neck, talked nostalgically about steam engines, like a retired railwayman. 'I'll tell you', he said. 'The steam engine was basically a simple piece of machinery – boiler, fire, bloody great wheels, there was nothing you couldn't see on a steam engine just by looking. You could test everything on a steam engine – not like a diesel. I'll tell you something else. In the old days, nobody got into the driver's cab without permission. Now you get people using it as a short cut, jumping in one side and out the other.'

When pressed, they obliged by talking about politics: how vicious the Tories were, how indecent the Act was. They were visibly militant; they were, they said cheerfully, much more militant than they had been. One driver, described as the Conservative among them, said the reason men at commuter stations were so militant was that they saw the prosperous middle classes all the time. 'You see the buggers going off for their holidays a week before the bank holiday', he said. 'You see the buggers coming back a week after.' A minute later they were talking about engines again. They were easily identified as militants; just as easily identified as craftsmen unhappy at the decay of their craft. In the end, what they most wanted to talk about was work.

8. Balance of Power

The dockers' dispute of 1972 was one of those issues that spring to life as though nature had intended them to illustrate complicated arguments that few ordinary people could otherwise be bothered to listen to. Years of talk about the power of the unions crystallized into a series of events that showed one group of workers to have every appearance of power. Authority was seen to back away hastily, its wig slipping over one ear; boots and fists flew on television screens; new concessions to the dockers were produced almost daily. Everyone heard about the plight of their declining industry. But the way they set about seeking more money and security was not at all as the British worker was supposed to behave. Their attitude to the law, as embodied in the Industrial Relations Act, was anarchic. Militant dockers, with the support of militants elsewhere, were apparently aflame to alter the balance of forces between unions and State, in favour of the unions. To put it another way, the question arose of whether the dockers, and behind them all the other militants, might not be trying to change some basic assumptions about social rights and rewards. The issue became concrete, in a way it had not been before.

Even the skeleton of the dispute is unwieldy. Basic changes in cargo-handling during the 1960s, in particular the use of containers, sharply reduced the demand for dock workers. Most container traffic is packed at its source inland and not opened until its destination. About one-seventh is made up of part-loads and so is available for dockers. Some of it goes to workers outside the docks. This tiny fraction of traffic that could be packed by dockers, but isn't, is the root of the trouble. Past circumstances have made dockers jealous of their rights. They used to be casual labour, hired by the day; this lasted until 1967. In later years they were protected against the worst of the system by being enrolled on a register of dock workers, with guaranteed wages. 'Registered dockers' have the legal right to handle all cargo within the docks, but no rights outside. As containers flourished and traditional dock-work dwindled, the men wanted to keep as much of the new work as possible. But they were unable to have work being done at depots near the docks reserved for them. This suited firms who were none too keen on employing dockers, with their reputation for thieving, laziness and general awkwardness. Dockers' resentment at losing work that might have been theirs (though they exaggerated the amount that could be saved) was all the worse because some of the new depots beyond their reach were operated by former employers.

The decline in dock labour, from 65,000 to 42,000 in the last seven years, is severe, but comparable to that in coal-mining or on the railways. But dockers are a comparatively small group, clannish and inward-looking. The harsh conditions that made them underdogs now arouse sympathy; at the same time, they are no longer underdogs in the old sense, and their tradition of closeness and toughness gives them a physical presence that is psychologically useful in confrontations. In this they resemble the miners; they are angry men it is best to leave alone; they demand a little sympathy for the brutality of their past and induce a little fear for their determination today.

By 1972 there had been many quarrels about containers, and no final settlement. In March, Liverpool dockers were disputing the right of some cargo-handling firms to employ whom they liked. Lorries were being blacked. One family-owned business, Heaton's Transport, took the matter to the new Industrial Relations Court. The court found that the dockers were improperly inducing Heaton's lorries to break their contract. The men's union, the TGWU, was not registered under the Act, and so the lorry-blacking was an unfair industrial practice. The courts said it must stop; Jack Jones wrote to say the union would not be represented, and on 29 March the court fined the union £5,000 for contempt. Three weeks later, with the lorries still blacked, the union was fined a further £50,000; this was the judgement that arrived in time to unnerve the railwaymen.

The T G W U was dismayed to be held responsible for the actions of its shop stewards in Liverpool. The union executive agonized for hours about whether to pay the fine or risk having its assets seized, and Jones is said to have had a bare majority for taking the prudent course. The money was paid on 2 May, forty-eight hours before the time-limit expired.

Belatedly appearing in court to defend itself against continuing complaints by Heaton's, the T G W U argued unsuccessfully that it was not responsible for its shop stewards, and was given three weeks to discipline them. Union officials told them to stop, but they took no notice, and Jones was not prepared to go further. He said in public that 'it will always be the policy of this union to defend shop stewards operating within the terms of established agreements. Provided that is done, we will defend to the end the right of shop stewards to exercise their responsibilities.' A local dispute had become a national confrontation. One result was that dockers gave notice of a union-backed national strike; another was that talks began with the Government about the working rights of dockers. This was an issue that had to be faced, sooner or later; so was the relationship between a union and its shop stewards. Unlike the railway dispute, this one was ripe for the attentions of the Industrial Relations Court. But, as in the other case, events moved too fast for comfort.

The T G W U was temporarily taken off the hook when the Court of Appeal ruled in mid-June that in cases complained off, at Liverpool and Hull, the union was not, after all, responsible for the stewards, and Jack Jones could have his money back. The dock strike was postponed until the end of July, pending an inquiry into job-security headed by Jones and Lord Aldington, chairman of the Port of London Authority. It was now a dispute about broad political policy: to what extent should the Government intervene to secure the future of workers in a declining industry? Tension developed between the T G W U and its militants; this was unfortunate, in view of Jones's creed of shopfloor democracy. When the dockers' delegates were at the meeting that postponed the strike, a hundred or more militants demanding quick action picketed Transport House, the union headquarters, and invaded the meeting hall. Union leaders were called scabs and leeches. Officials refrained from calling the police, but put in a prompt order for a set of crowd-proof doors.

During the same week, a new and improbable episode came to a head, the case of Chobham Farm. This was a large container depot on Hackney Marshes, in east London. Dockers were picketing it with signs declaring 'Keep out! This depot is traditional dock work.' The container workers inside saw their jobs being sacrificed for the sake of peace, and stumbled rather half-heartedly into an application to the NIRC to restrain their fellow unionists from picketing. Tony Churchman, the shop steward at the depot, was more used to dealing with matters like soap for the washbasins or sugar for the tea. He says he aged ten years and started to go grey. The case arrived in court, and three named dockers were ordered to stop picketing. One of them was Bernie Steer, secretary of the National Port Shop Stewards Committee, the unofficial group of activists which was planning the blacking and picketing throughout Britain; another was Vic Turner, the committee's chairman. Picketing continued, a row of men leaning against a wall in the sun, under a banner that read:

> Royal Group of Docks
> Shop Stewards Committee
> Arise Ye Workers

Just as the three dockers were about to be arrested and gaoled for contempt, the Appeal Court, intervening again, set aside the committal order on the grounds that the evidence of contempt was unsatisfactory. The move was set in motion by the Official Solicitor (prompted by the NIRC), an obscure figure whose appearance was greeted with derision by the dockers. Turner, courting martyrdom, said it was a 'bloody liberty'.

This was not the end of the trouble at Chobham Farm. The company agreed to employ forty dockers. When they arrived on 10 July, some of the container men claimed they had been diverted to menial jobs, sweeping floors and cleaning lavatories. Counter-pickets of drivers and container men stopped incoming lorries, handing them scraps of paper that declared 'BROTHER. Dock workers have been employed here and depot workers replaced.' At another container depot nearby, policemen watched while docker-pickets asked lorries to go away, and container-pickets asked them to come in.

These antics were presently overshadowed by a new application to the court. An east London firm called Midland Cold Storage named seven docker-pickets, among them Steer and Turner. This time the evidence was meticulously assembled. Particular consignments of prawns, Chinese rabbits and boiler-suits had failed to arrive because of picketing. Two private detectives had driven a lorry up to the picket line, and recorded a conversation, which was played to the court. Evidence was given of the 'Cherry Blossom' blacking list, which noted the numbers of all lorries that crossed picket lines, and circulated them to other ports. Pickets were alleged to have told a driver that his van would be turned over on his next visit to Midland, and to have added: 'Remember, you can't drive with one arm.'

The climax might have been staged to cause maximum confusion. On 7 July the court ordered the seven dockers to stop blacking vehicles at the Midland Cold Store. Steer said it was 'Just not on', adding blandly that 'we are simply members of the shop stewards' committee who carry out the wishes of the men'. Meanwhile the Aldington-Jones committee was hurrying to prepare its report; and the House of Lords was considering an appeal by Heaton's and others, against the Appeal Court's ruling the month before, that the T G W U was not responsible for its shop stewards in Liverpool and Hull. On 20 July, Midland Cold Storage pressed its complaint against Steer and the rest for continued blacking, and the following day five of them were arrested and gaoled for contempt. Militants in many unions hoped that this marked the beginning of open industrial conflict over the Act. The dockers went on unofficial strike, supported spasmodically by a hundred thousand other workers, among them busmen, lorry drivers, meat and vegetable porters and printers, who succeeded in stopping national newspapers for four days. Strikers marched from Fleet Street to the T U C in Bloomsbury and then up to north London and Pentonville Prison, chanting 'Free the dockers! Tories out!'

The five dockers went to gaol on a Friday. On the next Wednesday the T U C called for a one-day national strike the following week; the motion was proposed by Hugh Scanlon and seconded by Jack Jones. It would have been the first of its kind since 1926, but the plans were undone almost at once. The House of Lords allowed the Heaton's appeal, thus restoring the In- dustrial Court's original verdict. Later the same day the five dockers were released by the NIRC, on the grounds that since the union was now finally held responsible for its shop stewards, it was time to make a fresh start. Legal eyebrows were raised at this turn of events. Steer, Turner and the others popped out of gaol, announcing that they had won another victory. The militants' cup brimmed over when the Aldington-Jones interim report, regarded as unsatisfactory, was rejected by the docks delegates. By the end of the week an official national docks strike had begun. The TGWU was poorer by £55,000, with legal costs estimated at another £25,000, and it was open to fresh actions by shippers and hauliers. The lorry-blacking continued, but for the moment this particular tiger lay dormant. The day when the next firm would go to court, armed with the Lords decision, still lay in the future, though probably at no great distance. While Aldington and Jones revised their report, seeking more assur- ances about jobs from employers and the Government, dockers busied themselves picketing unregistered ports, outside the national scheme. Busloads of them rushed up and down the east coast, using mobility and careful planning, as the miners had done earlier in the year. Lorries were attacked and police injured in violent incidents at wharves near Scunthorpe. At Richborough in Kent two coasters had their moorings cut at night.

But the best-publicized violence was reserved for the TGWU. On 15 August new Aldington-Jones proposals were published. These included plans for port authorities to surcharge containers not packed by dockers, and for investigating the unregistered ports, both of which appeared to have the Government's blessing. The docker's delegates met at Transport House on 16 August, and decided to call off the strike. This infuriated militants who were jammed into Smith Square outside. Delegates were chased and threatened as they left. A police inspector, remonstrating with a pursuer, was told: 'The only way we can get through to these bastards is to terrorize them.' Twenty or thirty men entered Transport House, and found Jack Jones and two colleagues holding a press conference in a third-floor committee room. He was accused of selling out the dockers. Water, a metal ash-can and a torn-up union card were thrown at him. A docker who said his subscription had helped pay for the building shouted that it was 'like buying a house for the man who crucified Jesus'. Then the reporters were called capitalist hacks and bundled out. Jones remained to talk with the dockers, while in the street others continued to simmer, alternately threatening the television cameras and being interviewed for them. 'Smash this fucking lot up, that's what we want to do,' one man said comprehensively. A Hull docker sharpened the sense of violence by telling his interviewer: 'I'm afraid you don't know what violence is, my friend.'

Jones came out of it well, playing down the ugly moments and insisting that the trouble-makers were not representative. A few days later militants failed to persuade mass meetings of dockers to reject the Aldington-Jones proposals, and the strike ended. The real issues, though, showed little change.

What mattered most was not the Act but the situations the Act sought to deal with. The dockers were there anyway, insisting that the world owed them a better living. Their average earnings, by 1972, were between £40 and £45 for a week of forty hours or less. If no work was available for them, they would join a 'temporary unattached register' (usually containing well under 1,000 men) and draw £20 a week from an employers' fund. A docker who chose to leave the industry could take up to £2,300 severance pay; this was raised to £4,000 during the Aldington-Jones talks. By the standards of the day, they were not badly served.

They had a genuine sense of grievance against employers who spirited jobs away from under their noses. They saw property developers at work for large profits on the decayed wharves and warehouses. They knew that Midland Cold Storage was part of the Vestey empire. But even their grievances against the exigencies of change in a capitalists' world had to be qualified. Many employers said they had good reason for wanting to be rid of dock workers. The head of Midland said: 'Dockers have literally forced business out of the port of London through their restrictive practices and high rates.'* More often employers said it in private for fear of repercussions, but they made no bones about too much money for too little work. One analysis of unidentified dockers at work over a six-week period in 1968 is quoted in a recent book.† About 45 per cent of the 9.2 hours attended by the men each day were lost for avoidable reasons (such as bad timekeeping) or wasteful practices. Ten per cent were lost through weather. Less than half the working day was productive. The counter-pickets at Chobham Farm would tell anyone who cared to listen what rogues the dockers were. 'My own brother was a docker,' said one. 'He was in the hold of a ship, unloading frozen lamb's carcasses. One slipped off the hook and came down and missed him by a hairsbreadth – but it missed him. He got £75 in "frightened money". That's ridiculous.' The old charge of systematic pilfering lingers on. The Port of London Authority mumble and go red with embarrassment when asked about it. Old dockers say it used to happen because men had to thieve to live. A young freight-company executive who wouldn't name his company for fear I identified it described how coloured television sets could disappear from the docks. He said his previous firm imported sausages from Poland. Every consignment contained damaged crates and missing sausages; it was a fact of life; the company would agree a figure with the port authorities and deduct it from the bill for warehousing.

On another occasion I met an ex-docker who talked freely and not defensively about thieving. It was the tradition, he said: as long as it was thieving from the capitalists, that was all right. He was distanced from it; he stood outside the docks and looked in at their private world. 'If you drink a few bottles of Scotch from a cargo of two hundred tons, what's it matter?' he said. 'To break a gas meter would have been an enormous sin, but nobody suffered as a result of robbing a wharf, especially when you saw hundreds of tons of stuff rotting – tomatoes going bad and potatoes going to seed to keep the price up. What do a few

*The *Observer*, 30 July 1972.

†*Dockers: the Impact of Industrial Change*, David F. Wilson; Fontana/Collins; p. 253.

bottles of Scotch matter? The docks were a very moral society in other ways. If someone was sick down the street, everybody would march in to help. It was a very intense way of life. You have to measure this against the trivial nature of the thieving.'

What the Act did was to provide a framework for publicizing the troubles of the docks and forcing them towards a conclusion. The unions had dithered for years over containers. The men's grievances grew, and so did the gap between their mood and that of their officials. In raking through so many hot coals, the Act stirred up anger and bitterness; this is another way of looking at it. Attitudes certainly hardened, and that was generally held to be unfortunate. But for all the soft words about seeing the other person's point of view, the intention of the Act was to decide certain issues in terms of power. Attitudes were meant to harden. Sir John Donaldson, president of the Industrial Court rebuked both T G W U and employers for not taking action against dockers. In a judgement on 18 May he asked why a company called North Sea Ferries had done nothing against dockers it employed, and said: 'The short answer is that, like the union, they were afraid to do so. In this they are not alone, for we know of no employer in a similar position who has taken any action.' Replying to counsel's point that North Sea Ferries had decided discretion was the better part of valour, Donaldson said that 'courage and leadership and an ability to distinguish between discretion and short-term expediency' were needed. This sounded a clear encouragement to faint-hearted companies. The Act, as the unions complained during its progress into law, is not there for nothing.

The matter of a union and its shop stewards was ready and waiting for the Act. Jack Jones argues for 'genuine decentralization' as a means of producing better local agreements and higher wages. 'A union executive can guide, it can lead, it can persuade, it can coordinate. What it cannot do is to bully or instruct.'* Others (like Hugh Scanlon) are more explicit about shopfloor democracy. The movement to give workers a voice in their affairs shades into the movement to acquire power through every twist and turn of the local situation. Jones in no way condoned the

*The *Sunday Times*, 23 April 1972.

dockers' violence, nor can he have wanted to see the situation drift out of his union's influence, as it did at times. But his industrial philosophy is part of the network of ideas that leaves workers free to defend or better themselves as they think best. The union didn't decide on picketing and lorry-blacking; that was left to shop stewards, some of them in the T G W U and some of them not. Donaldson said the union was afraid to act against its own members; it is more plausible to suggest that the union's philosophy was of a kind to make it unwilling, rather than afraid. The T G W U's counsel said in court that the union, having considered withdrawing the stewards' credentials, had decided this would only make a bad situation worse. No doubt it would have done, given the relationship that existed between union and stewards. But this relationship wasn't an act of God. It reflected something of the philosophy of the union. The T G W U's leaders may have wanted to call off the blacking in the particular circumstances. But it was a bit late in the day. Shopfloor democracy is a deliberate movement, not an accident. An article by two advocates of workers' control in 1969 remarked that

the present campaign in the docks industry has reached the stage of arguing that control of the docks must be extended to include control over the new inland container terminals, whose private owners will by-pass, and thus subvert, the dockers' control in the established ports, if they are left untouched.*

This is how the container issue appears to militants. It was there before the Act. All the Act did was to say that the militants' behaviour must now be legally justified in terms of a set of rules, laid down for the general good.

The trade-union movement has resisted the Act because it believes itself threatened. There has been much argument as to whether any group is entitled to reject a law on the grounds that it is unfair or wrong-headed. Since this group consists theoretically of nearly half the country's workers, the argument is both bizarre and impracticable. If the trade unions refuse to accept the Industrial Relations Act, it will be unworkable. It is by no means certain that the unions will refuse. But if they do reject

Marxism Today, Ken Coates and Tony Topham, January 1969.

the equilibrium of forces between unions and State that is implied by the Act, then the equation will have to work itself out in some other form. This equilibrium is the real issue. It incorporates all the mainstream assumptions of British society. Unions have a right to exist, to seek higher pay and better conditions, and to withdraw their labour. They have a right to cause inconvenience as long as it is moderate inconvenience. They are entitled to put in wage claims every year as long as they are reasonable wage claims. They may talk to their hearts' content about industrial democracy as long as the democratic machine, like the democratic machine in society at large, votes in terms of acceptable alternatives.

But in the last ten or fifteen years, the unions and their members – not all, certainly, but enough to make a difference – have begun to challenge and re-interpret what is 'moderate', 'reasonable' and 'acceptable'. A union leader like Lawrence Daly will see this as a striving for the light. The average employer will see it as short-sighted greed and self-interest. But it is undoubtedly happening. The unions seek a new equilibrium, in which their position is stronger. The dockers offer an extreme version, almost a caricature, of this process. The Industrial Relations Act recognized that in any encounter the unions were protected by the law and insufficiently controlled by it, a legacy of the days when the workers were in no shape to challenge authority. Almost from the start it proved its point by the way the blackers and pickets went happily ahead, blacking and picketing. Determined dockers could damage a company whose policies they disagreed with, just as determined miners could force the Government to pay them money it had publicly committed itself to refusing. Change on the docks could be modified in favour of the dockers, not because of rational argument but because of militant action. The Act crystallized situations. It demonstrated the power of groups of workers. The Act having gone so far, it seems inconceivable not to use it further, unless it's to be dismantled and put away.

These are gloomy alternatives. One hints at repression, the other at anarchy. The other option is to recognize a case for giving the unions more of what they want, not at gunpoint but as a matter of social justice. Perhaps the world does owe the dockers a better living. It is not a very helpful suggestion. The amount of extra money and participation available is strictly limited within the existing economic system. Fat wage increases for everyone will produce roaring inflation and instability, throwing us all into a melting pot; excellent for those who wish to be melted, disagreeable for those who don't. But if wage claims are to be contained, how will this be done? The alternatives here are disagreeable, too. Legislation will produce unrest and strikes, with further perilous work for the Act. It is a scenario for trouble. The best hope is that the more moderate unions, confronted with a desperate situation, might seek a reconciliation with the Government, and by so doing draw on the reserves of moderation that doubtless exist. That sounds like wishful thinking. Compromises must lie ahead for all parties. But it would be fanciful to suppose that the unions will subside and become what they were twenty years ago.